SAFE AND SECURE

A Senior's Guide to Avoiding Scams

Ricky Roane

Safe and Secure: A Senior's Guide to Avoiding Scams

Author: Ricky Roane

Publisher: Talesmith Studio

Paperback ISBN: 979-8-218-46713-5

First Edition 2024

To Gretel,

In loving memory of a funny, kindhearted soul who embraced everyone with love and warmth. Your Christian faith and boundless kindness continue to inspire those who knew you. This book is dedicated to you, a beacon of light and love in our lives.

With heartfelt gratitude,

Ricky

About the author

Ricky Roane

Ricky Roane is a distinguished cyber security executive, dedicated leader, and USAF veteran with over 22 years of experience in Information Technology and Security. As the Founder and CEO of both Adversary Mindset and Auventic, Inc., Ricky has been at the forefront of offensive security and AI safety, ensuring that technology enhances, rather than overshadows, human potential.

Ricky's expertise in cyber security is extensive and unparalleled. He has led and performed advanced adversary Red Team digital and physical operations, orchestrated enterprise penetration tests, identified zero-day vulnerabilities in commercial and open-source software, and conducted comprehensive security architecture reviews. His work spans a variety of industries, including financial, aerospace, U.S. federal government, U.S. military, and health-care sectors.

Ricky's extensive background, hands-on experience, and unwavering dedication make him uniquely qualified to educate and protect seniors from the growing threat of scams and fraud. His approach combines technical expertise with a genuine passion for making a significant impact, ensuring that your loved ones receive the best guidance and protection available.

Through his professional journey and personal dedication, Ricky Roane has demonstrated his capability and commitment to safeguarding individuals and organizations from cyber threats. His book, "Safe and Secure: A Senior's Guide to Avoiding Scams," is a testament to his expertise and a vital resource for those looking to protect their loved ones.

Contents

One

Introduction

♥

Hey there! If you're reading this, it means someone who loves you very much wants to help keep you safe from the many tricky scams out there. The internet is an amazing place, but it's also full of people who are up to no good. This guide is here to help you recognize and avoid those troublemakers, so you can enjoy all the good stuff the internet has to offer without any worries.

A Message from Your Loved Ones

Your family wants nothing but the best for you. They've seen how scams and frauds can hurt people, and they want to make sure you're protected. That's why they gave you this book. It's filled with easy-to-understand advice and tips to help you stay safe online and in everyday life. They know that navigating the modern world of technology can be daunting, but they're here to support you every step of the way. So, grab a cup of coffee, sit back, and let's get started on keeping you safe and secure!

How to Use This Guide

This guide is designed to be as straightforward and helpful as possible. Here's a quick rundown of what you'll find:

- **Understanding Common Scams:** Learn about the most common types of scams and how to spot them.

- **Safe Practices:** Practical tips to keep your

personal information secure.

- **Tools and Resources:** Recommendations for software and services that can help protect you.

- **Responding to a Threat:** Steps to take if you think you've been scammed.

- **Practical Scenarios and FAQs:** Real-life examples and answers to common questions.

- **Quizzes:** See how well you've retained what you've learned.

- **Appendices:** A helpful glossary of terms, a checklist for online safety, some quick tips for staying safe, and a list of additional resources.

Feel free to jump to any section that interests you. You don't have to read it all at once—take your time, and refer back to it whenever you need a refresher. Each chapter is packed with valuable information and designed to be easy to understand. Don't worry if you're not a tech expert; this guide is written with you in mind.

Why Cybersecurity Matters for Seniors

You might be wondering, "Why do I need to worry about scams?" Well, scammers often target seniors because they believe older adults might be less familiar with technology and more trusting of strangers. Scammers are constantly coming up with new tricks to deceive people, and they often see seniors as easy targets. But don't worry—this guide will help you become savvy about the common tricks scammers use and how to avoid them.

Think of this guide as a friendly companion that walks you through the maze of modern-day scams. By the time you finish reading, you'll feel more confident about identifying and dodging these scams like a pro. The internet and modern technology offer incredible benefits, but it's crucial to navigate them safely.

Real Stories, Real Consequences

To illustrate the importance of being scam-aware, let's look at a real-life story. Mary, a 72-year-old retiree, received a call from someone claiming to be from the IRS. The caller said she owed back taxes and threatened her with arrest if she didn't pay immediately. Scared and wanting to avoid trouble, Mary gave her bank account details over the phone. Unfortunately, the caller was a scammer, and Mary lost a significant amount of her savings.

Stories like Mary's are all too common. But with the knowledge you'll gain from this guide, you'll be equipped to recognize and respond to such threats, protecting yourself and your hard-earned money. Understanding these risks is the first step towards preventing them.

Let's also hear about John, who was excited when he got an email claiming he had won a lottery he didn't remember entering. The email looked legitimate, and the sender seemed credible. All John had to do was pay a small fee to cover the processing costs. Thrilled at the prospect of winning, he paid the fee, only to realize later that it was a scam and there was no lottery. John's excitement turned into frustration and disappointment. These stories underline the importance of being vigilant and cautious.

The Benefits of Staying Informed

Staying informed about scams isn't just about protecting yourself—it's also about peace of mind. Knowing how to spot a scam and what steps to take can save you from stress and financial loss. Plus, you'll be able to share this knowledge with friends and family, helping to keep them safe too. The more people who are aware of these threats, the harder it becomes for scammers to succeed.

Being knowledgeable means you can enjoy the convenience of technology without constant fear. It's about empowering yourself and those around you to use the internet and other technologies safely and securely.

A Journey Towards Safety

This guide is more than just a book; it's a journey towards greater safety and confidence in the digital age. We'll cover a wide range of topics, from phishing emails to phone scams, and provide you with practical tools to protect yourself. Each chapter is designed to be clear and easy to follow, with real-life examples and simple tips.

Remember, you're not alone in this journey. Your loved ones care deeply about your safety and have given you this guide as a way to show their support. So, take your time, read through the sections, and don't hesitate to reach out to them or other trusted sources if you have questions or need help. Every step you take towards understanding these threats is a step towards a safer, more secure life.

Getting Started

Now that we've set the stage, it's time to dive into the first chapter. We'll start by exploring the different types of scams that are out there, helping you understand what to look for and how to stay safe. Ready? Let's get started!

Two

Understanding Common Scams

In today's world, scams have become increasingly sophisticated, targeting people from all walks of life. Scammers use clever tactics and emotional manipulation to deceive their victims. However, scammers often see seniors as prime targets, believing they may be less familiar with modern technology and more trusting of strangers. This chapter aims to arm you with the knowledge needed to recognize and avoid various scams. By understanding these threats, you can protect yourself and help others stay safe too.

Let's start by understanding why scammers target seniors specifically. Seniors are often perceived as more financially stable, having saved for retirement, and may not be as tech-savvy, making them easier to deceive. Moreover, the isolation that some seniors experience can make them more susceptible to scams, as they might be more willing to engage with strangers who show them attention or offer them seemingly good opportunities.

One important thing to remember is that scammers are experts at what they do. They use psychological tricks to create a sense of urgency, fear, or excitement to prompt immediate action. This manipulation can make even the most cautious individuals fall victim to their schemes. The good news is that by learning to recognize the common signs of scams, you can protect yourself and avoid becoming a victim.

In this chapter, we will cover various types of scams that you might encounter. These include:

- **Phishing Scams**

- **Email Scams**

- **Phone Scams**

- **Social Media Risks**

- **Identity Theft**

- **Investment Scams**

- **Lottery and Sweepstakes Scams**

- **Charity Scams**

- **Tech Support Scams**

- **Romance Scams**

- **Home Repair Scams**

Each section will provide detailed information on how these scams operate, the warning signs to look out for, and practical tips to protect yourself.

Why Being Informed is Your Best Defense

Staying informed is the best defense against scammers. Knowledge empowers you to spot the red flags and take appropriate action before it's too late. The more you know about how these scams work, the better prepared you will be to avoid them. Additionally, sharing this knowledge with friends and family can help create a community of informed individuals who look out for each other.

For instance, if you receive an unexpected email or phone call that seems suspicious, you'll know not to provide any personal information and to verify the source independently. If something seems too good to be true, it probably is. Trust your instincts and don't be afraid to hang up the phone or delete an email if it raises any red flags.

The Importance of Reporting Scams

Another crucial aspect of combating scams is reporting them. When you report a scam, you not only protect yourself but also help prevent others from falling victim. Authorities can use the information you provide to investigate and shut down fraudulent operations. We'll cover how to report scams in detail in a later chapter, but for now, remember that your vigilance and willingness to report suspicious activities can make a significant difference.

A Personal Commitment to Safety

Finally, protecting yourself from scams requires a personal commitment to safety. This means staying informed, being cautious with your personal information, and continually educating yourself about new threats. Scammers are always evolving their tactics, so it's important to stay one step ahead by being proactive about your safety.

As we delve into each type of scam, keep in mind that you have the power to protect yourself. Armed with the knowledge from this guide, you can navigate the digital world with confidence and peace of mind.

Phishing Scams

Imagine this: You receive an email that looks like it's from your bank. The email claims there's been suspicious activity on your account and urges you to click a link to verify your information. This is a classic example of phishing, where scammers pose as trusted entities to steal your personal information.

What is Phishing?

Phishing is a type of scam where attackers send fraudulent messages designed to trick you into revealing sensitive information. These messages often appear to come from legitimate sources, such as banks, credit card companies, or other trusted institutions. The goal is to steal personal data like login credentials, credit card numbers, or social security numbers.

Common Tactics Used in Phishing

Phishing scams can be highly sophisticated and convincing. Here are some common tactics scammers use:

- **Spoofed Email Addresses:** Scammers often create email addresses that closely resemble those of legitimate organizations. For example, instead of "yourbank.com," they might use "yourbank-security.com." Always check the sender's email address carefully.

- **Urgent Language:** Phishing emails often create a sense of urgency, using phrases like "immediate action required" or "your account will be suspended." This is meant to pressure you into acting quickly without thinking.

- **Generic Greetings:** Legitimate companies usually address you by name, while phishing emails might use greetings like "Dear Customer" or "Dear Sir/Madam." If an email doesn't address you personally, be cautious.

- **Suspicious Links:** Hover over any links in the email without clicking on them. The actual URL might be different from the displayed text, leading you to a fraudulent site. Scammers often use shortened URLs to disguise their true destination.

- **Attachments:** Phishing emails may include attachments that, when opened, can install malware on your device. Never open attachments from unknown or unexpected sources.

Real-Life Phishing Example

Let's consider the story of Alice. Alice received an email that seemed to be from her bank, warning her about a security breach. Panicked, she clicked the link provided in the email and was directed to a website that looked exactly like her bank's official site. Without thinking, she entered her login details. Shortly after, she noticed unauthorized transactions on her account. It turned out the email was a phishing scam, and the website was a fake designed to capture her login information.

Alice's story is a common one, but it's also preventable. By being aware of the tactics used by phishers and taking steps to verify the authenticity of such messages, you can avoid falling victim to these scams.

How to Recognize Phishing Attempts

Here are some key signs that an email or message might be a phishing attempt:

- **Unexpected Requests:** Be wary of unexpected requests for personal information, even if they appear to come from a trusted source.

- **Suspicious Links:** Avoid clicking on links in unsolicited emails. Instead, go directly to the website by typing the URL into your browser.

- **Spelling and Grammar Errors:** Many phishing emails contain spelling and grammar errors. Legitimate companies typically proofread their communications carefully.

- **Unusual Sender Address:** Check the sender's email address closely. Even a small discrepancy can indicate a phishing attempt.

Steps to Protect Yourself from Phishing Scams

1. **Verify the Sender:** If you receive an email that seems suspicious, contact the company directly using a known phone number or website to verify the message. Do not use any contact information provided in the suspicious email.

2. **Don't Click on Links:** Instead of clicking on links in emails, go directly to the website by typing the URL into your browser. This ensures you're visiting the legitimate site.

3. **Use Two-Factor Authentication:** Enable two-factor authentication (2FA) on your ac-

counts whenever possible. This adds an extra layer of security by requiring a second form of verification, such as a text message code.

4. **Install Antivirus Software:** Keep your antivirus software updated to protect against malware that might be delivered through phishing emails.

5. **Educate Yourself:** Stay informed about the latest phishing tactics and share this knowledge with friends and family to help protect them as well.

Reporting Phishing Scams

If you receive a phishing email, it's important to report it. Most email providers have a way to mark emails as phishing. Reporting these scams helps the providers improve their filters and protect other users. You can also report phishing attempts to organizations like the Federal Trade Commission (FTC) or the Anti-Phishing Working Group (APWG).

- **Email Provider:** Use the spam or phishing re- porting tools provided by your email service.

- **Federal Trade Commission (FTC):** File a complaint with the FTC at www.ftc.gov/com plaint.

- **Anti-Phishing Working Group (APWG):** For- ward phishing emails to reportphishing@ap wg.org.

Additional Resources for Learning About Phish- ing

- **StaySafeOnline:** This website offers re- sources and tips for recognizing and avoiding phishing scams – https://staysafeonline.org

- **FTC's Consumer Information:** The Federal Trade Commission provides information on how to identify and report phishing attempts – https://ReportFraud.ftc.gov

- **Anti-Phishing Working Group (APWG):** A global coalition focused on eliminating fraud

and identity theft caused by phishing and related attacks – https://apwg.org/reportphish
ing

By staying vigilant and following these tips, you can
protect yourself from phishing scams and keep your
personal information safe. Remember, it's always
better to take a moment to verify a message than
to rush and regret it later.

Email Based Scams

Email scams are a prevalent form of deception that
can take many shapes and forms. Scammers use
emails to trick you into giving up personal information or money. Understanding the different types of
email scams and their warning signs can help you
avoid falling victim to these schemes.

Lottery Scams

Imagine opening your inbox to find an email claiming you've won a lottery or prize. The email might look official, complete with logos and formal language. It states that you need to provide personal details or pay a small fee to claim your prize. However, this is a trap. The scammers are hoping you'll be excited enough to overlook the signs of a scam.

- **Warning Signs:** Unexpected lottery winnings, requests for personal information, payment of fees upfront.

- **How to Protect Yourself:** Remember, if you didn't enter a lottery, you can't win one. Legitimate lotteries do not ask for fees to claim prizes.

Inheritance Scams

Inheritance scams operate on a similar principle. You receive an email informing you that you're the beneficiary of a large inheritance from a distant relative. The email might come from a supposed lawyer or estate manager. To receive the inheritance, you must provide personal details or pay a processing fee.

- **Warning Signs:** Unexpected inheritance notices, requests for personal or financial information, urgency to act quickly.

- **How to Protect Yourself:** Verify the information independently. Contact your own lawyer or conduct a search to confirm the legitimacy.

Tech Support Scams

Tech support scams involve emails that claim there's a problem with your computer. The email might state that your computer is infected with a virus and that you need to call a tech support number provided in the email. Once you call, the scammer might try to gain remote access to your computer or ask for payment to fix non-existent issues.

- **Warning Signs:** Unsolicited tech support offers, urgency to fix issues, requests for remote access or payment.

- **How to Protect Yourself:** Legitimate tech support companies do not contact customers out of the blue. Always use known contact methods to reach out to tech support.

Real-Life Email Scam Examples

Let's look at the story of Robert. He received an email that seemed to come from a well-known lottery organization, stating that he had won a substantial amount of money. Excited, he followed the instructions and provided his bank details to pay a small processing fee. Soon after, he noticed unauthorized withdrawals from his account. The email was a scam, and Robert lost a significant sum of money.

Another example is Sarah, who received an email from a supposed tech support agent claiming her computer had a severe virus. Worried about her data, she called the provided number and allowed the scammer remote access to her computer. The scammer installed malware, which stole her personal information and locked her out of her device.

How to Recognize Email Scams

Here are some key signs that an email might be a scam:

- **Unexpected Requests:** Be wary of emails that ask for personal or financial information out of the blue.

- **Too Good to Be True:** Emails promising large sums of money, prizes, or inheritances are usually scams.

- **Spelling and Grammar Errors:** Many scam emails contain spelling and grammar mistakes. Legitimate companies usually proofread their communications carefully.

- **Suspicious Links and Attachments:** Avoid clicking on links or downloading attachments from unknown or unsolicited emails.

Steps to Protect Yourself from Email Scams

- **Verify the Sender:** If you receive an email that seems suspicious, contact the organization directly using a known phone number or website to verify the message. Do not use any contact information provided in the suspicious email.

- **Don't Click on Links or Attachments:** Instead of clicking on links or downloading attachments in emails, visit the website directly by typing the URL into your browser.

- **Use Email Filters:** Many email providers offer spam filters that can help detect and block scam emails. Make sure these filters are enabled and adjust them if necessary.

- **Report Suspicious Emails:** Most email services have options to mark emails as spam or phishing. Reporting these emails helps improve the provider's filters and protects other users.

Reporting Email Scams

If you receive an email scam, it's important to report it. Here's how you can do it:

- **Email Provider:** Use the spam or phishing reporting tools provided by your email service.

- **Federal Trade Commission (FTC):** File a complaint with the FTC at www.ftc.gov/com plaint.

- **Anti-Phishing Working Group (APWG):** Forward phishing emails to reportphishing@ap wg.org.

Additional Resources for Learning About Email Scams

- **StaySafeOnline:** Offers resources and tips for recognizing and avoiding email scams at https://staysafeonline.org/.

- **FTC's Consumer Information:** Provides information on how to identify and report email scams at https://reportfraud.ftc.gov/.

- **Anti-Phishing Working Group (APWG):** A global coalition focused on eliminating fraud and identity theft caused by phishing and related attacks at https://apwg.org/reportphishing/.

By staying vigilant and following these tips, you can protect yourself from email scams and keep your personal information safe. Remember, it's always better to take a moment to verify an email than to rush and regret it later.

***

Phone Scams

Phone scams are another prevalent form of fraud where scammers use telephone calls to deceive victims into providing personal information or money. These scams can be highly convincing, as scammers often impersonate trusted organizations or individuals to gain your trust.

Impersonation Scams

In impersonation scams, the caller pretends to be someone you trust, such as a government official, a bank representative, or a tech support agent. They might claim there's an urgent problem that requires your immediate action, such as a lawsuit, unpaid taxes, or a compromised bank account.

- **Warning Signs:** Unexpected calls from supposed officials, requests for personal infor-

mation, threats of legal action or arrest, demands for immediate payment.

- **How to Protect Yourself:** Hang up and verify
the caller's identity by contacting the organization directly using a known phone number.
Legitimate entities will not pressure you for
immediate payment or threaten you with arrest over the phone.

Prize and Lottery Scams

Prize and lottery scams involve a caller informing
you that you've won a prize or lottery. To claim
the prize, they ask for personal details or a fee to
cover processing or delivery costs. The excitement
of winning can make it easy to overlook the signs of
a scam.

- **Warning Signs:** Unexpected prize notifications, requests for personal information or
fees, urgency to act quickly.

- **How to Protect Yourself:** Remember, if you
didn't enter a contest, you can't win. Legit-

imate lotteries do not ask for fees to claim prizes. Verify any claims by contacting the organization directly.

Charity Scams

Charity scams exploit your goodwill by pretending to be charitable organizations seeking donations. These scammers often appear during times of crisis, such as natural disasters, to tug at your heartstrings and prompt immediate donations.

- **Warning Signs:** Unsolicited donation requests, high-pressure tactics, lack of information about the charity.

- **How to Protect Yourself:** Verify the legitimacy of the charity by checking with charity watchdog organizations like Charity Navigator or the Better Business Bureau. Legitimate charities will provide clear information and will not pressure you into donating immediately.

Text Message Scams

Text message scams, also known as SMS phishing or "smishing," aim to steal your personal information or money by pretending to be legitimate entities. These scams often involve messages that appear to be from trusted sources, such as banks, government agencies, or well-known companies, urging you to take immediate action.

- **Warning Signs:** Unsolicited text messages from unknown numbers. Messages claiming urgent issues that require immediate action, such as verifying account details or resolving a problem. Requests for personal information, passwords, or financial details. Links to unfamiliar or suspicious websites. Poor grammar or spelling errors.

- **How to Protect Yourself: Do Not Respond:** Ignore unsolicited text messages from unknown senders. Do not reply or click on any links. **Verify the Sender:** If the message claims to be from a known entity, contact the organization directly using a verified phone number or website to confirm the message's legitimacy. **Avoid Clicking Links:** Refrain from clicking on links in suspicious messages. Instead, type the organization's official website address into your browser. **Use Security Software:** Install and update security software on your mobile device to detect and block malicious messages. **Report Suspicious Messages:** Forward the scam message to your mobile carrier (usually by texting it to 7726) and report it to the Federal Trade Commission (FTC) at www.ftc.gov.

Real-Life Phone Scam Examples

Consider the story of Michael, who received a call from someone claiming to be from the IRS. The caller said he owed back taxes and threatened him with arrest if he didn't pay immediately. Panicked, Michael provided his bank account details and lost a significant amount of money. The call was a scam, and Michael had been tricked into giving away his personal information.

Another example is Linda, who received a call from a supposed charity seeking donations for disaster relief. Moved by the caller's story, she provided her credit card information over the phone. Later, she discovered unauthorized charges on her account and realized the call had been a scam.

How to Recognize Phone Scams

Here are some key signs that a phone call might be a scam:

- **Unexpected Calls:** Be cautious of unsolicited calls, especially from unknown numbers.

- **Urgent or Threatening Language:** Scammers often use threats or create a sense of urgency to pressure you into acting quickly.

- **Requests for Personal Information:** Legitimate organizations will not ask for sensitive information over the phone.

- **Too Good to Be True Offers:** Promises of prizes or money that seem too good to be true are usually scams.

Steps to Protect Yourself from Phone Scams

1. **Verify the Caller:** If you receive a suspicious call, hang up and contact the organization directly using a known phone number.

2. **Don't Provide Personal Information:** Never give out personal or financial information over the phone unless you are sure of the caller's identity.

3. **Register with the Do Not Call List:** This can help reduce the number of unsolicited calls you receive. You can register your phone number with the National Do Not Call Registry at www.donotcall.gov.

4. **Use Call Blocking Features:** Many phones and phone services offer call blocking features to help filter out unwanted calls.

5. **Report Suspicious Calls:** Report scam calls to the Federal Trade Commission (FTC) at www.ftc.gov/complaint and to your phone service provider.

Reporting Phone Scams

If you receive a phone scam, it's important to report it. Here's how you can do it:

- **Federal Trade Commission (FTC):** File a complaint with the FTC at www.ftc.gov/com plaint.

- **National Do Not Call Registry:** Report unwanted calls at www.donotcall.gov.

- **Local Law Enforcement:** If the scam involves threats or extortion, contact your local police department.

Additional Resources for Learning About Phone Scams

- **FTC's Consumer Information:** Provides information on how to identify and report phone scams at https://reportfraud.ftc.gov/.

- **AARP Fraud Watch Network:** Offers resources and tips for recognizing and avoiding phone scams at https://www.aarp.org/money/scams-fraud/about-fraud-watch-network/.

By staying vigilant and following these tips, you can protect yourself from phone scams and keep your personal information safe. Remember, it's always better to hang up on a suspicious call than to risk your safety or financial security.

Social Media Risks

Social media platforms are a great way to stay connected with friends and family, but they also come with risks. Scammers use these platforms to gather personal information, spread malware, and trick people into revealing sensitive data. Understanding these risks and knowing how to protect yourself can help you enjoy social media safely

Friend Requests from Strangers

Scammers often send friend requests from fake accounts. Once you accept, they can access your personal information and photos. They might use this information to steal your identity or create a fake profile that looks like yours.

- **Warning Signs:** Friend requests from people you don't know, profiles with few photos or information, overly generic or stolen photos.

- **How to Protect Yourself:** Only accept friend requests from people you know. Check the profile for signs of authenticity before accepting.

Suspicious Messages

You might receive messages from friends whose accounts have been hacked, or from strangers asking for help or money. These messages often contain links that lead to phishing sites or malware down-loads.

- **Warning Signs:** Messages asking for money or personal information, links that seem out of context, messages that create a sense of urgency.

- **How to Protect Yourself:** Verify the message by contacting the friend through another method, such as a phone call. Avoid clicking on suspicious links.

Fake Accounts

Scammers create fake profiles to impersonate someone you know. They might send you a friend request or message, trying to trick you into giving them money or personal information.

- **Warning Signs:** You are already friends with this person, profiles with minimal activity, recent account creation, and generic or stolen photos.

- **How to Protect Yourself:** Verify the identity

of the person by asking a question only they would know. Report fake accounts to the social media platform.

Real-Life Social Media Scam Examples

Consider the story of Karen, who received a friend request from what appeared to be an old classmate. After accepting the request, she received a message asking for help with a financial emergency. Wanting to help, Karen sent money through a wire transfer. Later, she discovered that the account was fake and she had been scammed.

Another example is Tom, who received a message from a friend's account asking him to click on a link to view photos. The link led to a phishing site that stole his login credentials. The scammer then used Tom's account to send similar messages to his friends, perpetuating the scam.

How to Recognize Social Media Risks

Here are some key signs that you might be dealing with a social media scam:

- **Unfamiliar Friend Requests:** Be cautious of friend requests from people you don't know or accounts with few details.

- **Urgent or Unusual Messages:** Messages that create a sense of urgency or ask for money are often scams.

- **Suspicious Links:** Avoid clicking on links in messages from unfamiliar sources or that seem out of context.

Steps to Protect Yourself from Social Media Scams

- **Adjust Privacy Settings:** Limit who can see your posts and personal information. Most social media platforms allow you to customize your privacy settings.

- **Verify Friend Requests:** Only accept friend

requests from people you know. Verify the identity of anyone who seems unfamiliar.

- **Be Cautious with Messages:** If you receive a suspicious message, verify it with the sender through another method. Avoid clicking on links or providing personal information.

- **Report Suspicious Activity:** Report fake accounts and suspicious messages to the social media platform. This helps protect you and other users.

- **Use Strong Passwords:** Ensure your social media accounts are protected with strong, unique passwords. Enable two-factor authentication (2FA) for added security.

Reporting Social Media Scams

If you encounter a social media scam, it's important to report it. Here's how you can do it:

- **Social Media Platform:** Use the platform's tools to report fake accounts, suspicious messages, and phishing attempts.

- **Federal Trade Commission (FTC):** File a complaint with the FTC at www.ftc.gov/complaint.

Additional Resources for Learning About Social Media Risks

- **StaySafeOnline:** Offers resources and tips for recognizing and avoiding social media scams.

- **FTC's Consumer Information:** Provides information on how to identify and report social media scams.

By staying vigilant and following these tips, you can protect yourself from social media scams and enjoy connecting with friends and family safely. Remember, it's always better to be cautious and verify information before taking action.

***

Identity Theft

Identity theft occurs when someone steals your personal information, such as your Social Security number, credit card number, or other identifying data, to commit fraud. This can lead to significant financial loss and damage to your credit. Understanding how identity theft happens and how to protect yourself is crucial in safeguarding your personal information.

Phishing and Spoofing

Scammers often use phishing emails and spoofed websites to trick you into revealing personal information. These emails and sites look legitimate but are designed to capture your data.

- **Warning Signs:** Unexpected requests for personal information, links to unfamiliar websites, urgent messages demanding immediate action.

- **How to Protect Yourself:** Verify the source

before providing any information. Avoid clicking on suspicious links or entering personal information on unfamiliar sites.

Data Breaches

Hackers may target companies that store your personal information, such as banks, retailers, and healthcare providers. When these companies are breached, your data can be stolen and used for fraudulent activities.

- **Warning Signs:** Notifications from companies about data breaches, unexpected changes in your accounts or credit report.

- **How to Protect Yourself:** Monitor your accounts regularly for suspicious activity. Consider using a credit monitoring service to alert you to potential fraud.

Mail Theft

Identity thieves might steal your mail to obtain personal information, such as bank statements, credit card offers, and tax documents.

- **Warning Signs:** Missing mail, unexpected changes in your mail delivery, unauthorized mail forwarding.

- **How to Protect Yourself:** Use a locked mailbox or a P.O. box. Shred sensitive documents before disposing of them.

Skimming

Skimming devices can be attached to ATMs, gas pumps, and point-of-sale terminals to capture your card information when you swipe.

- **Warning Signs:** Unusual devices attached to card readers, difficulty inserting your card.

- **How to Protect Yourself:** Inspect card readers before use. Use ATMs in well-lit, secure locations. Use cash instead of credit cards when feasible.

Real-Life Identity Theft Examples

Consider the story of Lisa, who noticed unauthorized charges on her credit card statement. After investigating, she discovered that her card information had been stolen through a skimming device at a gas station. Lisa had to go through the lengthy process of disputing the charges and securing her accounts.

Another example is James, who received a call from his bank about suspicious activity on his account. It turned out that his personal information had been stolen in a data breach at a retailer he frequently shopped at. James had to take immediate action to protect his identity and prevent further fraud.

How to Recognize Identity Theft

Here are some key signs that you might be a victim of identity theft:

- **Unexpected Charges:** Unauthorized charges on your bank or credit card statements.

- **New Accounts:** Unfamiliar accounts or loans on your credit report.

- **Missing Mail:** Expected mail not arriving, especially financial statements or bills.

- **Debt Collection Calls:** Calls from debt collectors about debts you don't recognize.

Steps to Protect Yourself from Identity Theft

- **Monitor Your Accounts:** Regularly check your bank and credit card statements for unauthorized transactions.

- **Check Your Credit Reports:** Review your credit reports annually from all three major credit bureaus (Equifax, Experian, TransUnion) to spot any unfamiliar accounts or activity.

- **Use Strong Passwords:** Protect your online

accounts with strong, unique passwords. Enable two-factor authentication (2FA) wherever possible.

- **Shred Sensitive Documents:** Shred any documents containing personal information before disposing of them.

- **Secure Your Mail:** Use a locked mailbox or a P.O. box to receive sensitive mail. Opt for electronic statements when possible.

What to Do If Your Identity Is Stolen

If you suspect your identity has been stolen, take immediate action:

- **Place a Fraud Alert:** Contact the three major credit bureaus to place a fraud alert on your credit report. This makes it harder for thieves to open accounts in your name.

- **Review Your Credit Reports:** Check your credit reports for any unauthorized accounts or activity.

- **Close Fraudulent Accounts:** Contact the companies where the fraud occurred and close the accounts. Request that they send you written confirmation.

- **File a Police Report:** Report the identity theft to your local police department.

- **Report to the FTC:** File a complaint with the Federal Trade Commission (FTC) at www.ide ntitytheft.gov. The FTC can help you create a recovery plan.

Reporting Identity Theft

Reporting identity theft is crucial to stopping further fraud. Here's how you can do it:

- **Credit Bureaus:** Contact Equifax, Experian, or TransUnion to place a fraud alert or credit freeze on your account.

- **Federal Trade Commission (FTC):** File a report with the FTC at www.identitytheft.gov.

- **Local Law Enforcement:** File a report with

your local police department to document the theft.

Additional Resources for Learning About Identity Theft

- **IdentityTheft.gov:** The FTC's resource for identity theft victims, offering recovery plans and reporting tools at https://www.identityt heft.gov.

- **StaySafeOnline:** Offers resources and tips for recognizing and avoiding identity theft at https://staysafeonline.org/.

- **Consumer Financial Protection Bureau (CFPB):** Provides information on how to protect yourself from identity theft at https://w ww.consumerfinance.gov/.

By staying vigilant and following these tips, you can protect yourself from identity theft and secure your personal information. Remember, taking proactive steps is essential in preventing identity theft and mitigating its impact if it occurs.

Investment Scams

Investment scams prey on individuals by promising high returns with little or no risk. These scams can be particularly devastating, as they often lead to significant financial losses. Understanding the different types of investment scams and their warning signs can help you protect your hard-earned money.

Ponzi Schemes

Ponzi schemes are fraudulent investment operations where returns are paid to earlier investors using the capital of newer investors. The scheme relies on a constant influx of new investments to continue paying returns, making it unsustainable in the long run.

- **Warning Signs:** Guaranteed high returns with little risk, overly consistent returns, secretive or complex investment strategies, difficulty receiving payments.

- **How to Protect Yourself:** Be wary of investments that promise high returns with little risk. Research the investment and the person offering it. Verify credentials with financial regulatory bodies.

Pyramid Schemes

Pyramid schemes involve recruiting individuals to invest money with the promise of earning high returns through the recruitment of others. The structure resembles a pyramid, with each new recruit required to invest money that is then used to pay earlier participants.

- **Warning Signs:** Emphasis on recruiting new participants, lack of a genuine product or service, complex commission structures.

- **How to Protect Yourself:** Avoid investments

that focus more on recruitment than on the sale of a legitimate product or service. Research the company and its business model.

Pump and Dump Schemes

In pump and dump schemes, scammers artificially inflate the price of a stock through false or misleading statements. Once the stock price is high enough, the scammers sell their shares at a profit, causing the price to plummet and leaving other investors with worthless stock.

- **Warning Signs:** Unsolicited stock tips, pressure to invest quickly, dramatic increases in stock price without clear reasons.

- **How to Protect Yourself:** Be cautious of unsolicited investment offers. Research the stock and the company before investing. Look for independent verification of claims.

Advance Fee Fraud

Advance fee fraud involves promising investors a significant return on their investment, provided they pay a fee upfront. Once the fee is paid, the scammer disappears, and the promised returns never materialize.

- **Warning Signs:** Requests for upfront fees, promises of guaranteed returns, lack of verifiable information about the investment.

- **How to Protect Yourself:** Never pay upfront fees for investment opportunities. Verify the legitimacy of the investment and the person offering it.

Real-Life Investment Scam Examples

Consider the story of Joe, who was approached by a friend with an exciting investment opportunity in a new technology company. The company promised high returns with minimal risk, and Joe decided to invest a significant amount of his savings. Initially, the returns seemed great, but soon after, the company collapsed, and Joe lost his investment. It turned out to be a Ponzi scheme.

Another example is Linda, who received an unsolicited email promoting a "can't-miss" stock tip. She invested in the stock, only to watch its value plummet shortly after. The stock had been artificially inflated in a pump and dump scheme, and Linda was left with a worthless investment.

How to Recognize Investment Scams

Here are some key signs that an investment opportunity might be a scam:

- **Unsolicited Offers:** Be wary of unsolicited investment offers, especially those that come through email, social media, or phone calls.

- **Guaranteed High Returns:** Promises of high returns with little or no risk are often too good to be true.

- **Pressure to Invest Quickly:** Scammers often create a sense of urgency to pressure you into making a quick decision.

- **Lack of Verifiable Information:** If you can't verify the investment details or the credentials of the person offering it, it's likely a scam.

Steps to Protect Yourself from Investment Scams

- **Research the Investment:** Before investing, thoroughly research the investment opportunity. Look for independent sources of information and verify the credentials of the person offering the investment.

- **Ask Questions:** Don't be afraid to ask detailed questions about the investment. Legitimate investors will be transparent and willing to provide information.

- **Verify with Regulatory Bodies:** Check with financial regulatory bodies, such as the Securities and Exchange Commission (SEC) or your local financial regulator, to ensure the investment and the person offering it are legitimate.

- **Consult a Financial Advisor:** Seek advice from a trusted financial advisor before making any significant investments. They can help you assess the risks and benefits.

- **Avoid Upfront Fees:** Be cautious of any investment that requires upfront fees. Legitimate investments do not require you to pay fees before you start earning returns.

Reporting Investment Scams

If you suspect an investment scam, it's important to report it. Here's how you can do it:

- **Securities and Exchange Commission (SEC):** File a complaint with the SEC at www.sec.gov/complaint.

- **Financial Industry Regulatory Authority (FINRA):** Report investment scams to FINRA at www.finra.org.

- **Local Law Enforcement:** Contact your local police department to report investment fraud.

Additional Resources for Learning About Investment Scams

- **Investor.gov:** The SEC's resource for investors, offering tools and information to help you avoid fraud at https://www.investor.gov/.

- **FINRA's BrokerCheck:** A tool to verify the credentials of investment professionals and check for disciplinary actions at https://brokercheck.finra.org/.

- **AARP Fraud Watch Network:** Offers resources and tips for recognizing and avoiding investment scams at https://www.aarp.org/money/scams-fraud/about-fraud-watch-network/.

By staying vigilant and following these tips, you can protect yourself from investment scams and safeguard your financial future. Remember, if an investment opportunity sounds too good to be true, it probably is.

***

Lottery and Sweepstakes Scams

Lottery and sweepstakes scams exploit the excitement of winning a prize to trick victims into providing personal information or paying fees. These scams can appear highly convincing and often lead to significant financial losses. Knowing how these scams operate and recognizing their warning signs can help you avoid falling victim.

How Lottery and Sweepstakes Scams Work

In these scams, you receive a message—either by email, phone, or mail—claiming you've won a lottery or sweepstakes. The message might look official, complete with logos and formal language. It often states that to claim your prize, you need to provide personal information or pay a fee for taxes, processing, or shipping.

Advance Fee Scams

In advance fee scams, the scammer tells you that you need to pay a fee upfront to claim your prize. This fee might be for taxes, processing, or shipping. Once you pay the fee, the scammer disappears, and you never receive the prize.

- **Warning Signs:** Requests for upfront fees, promises of guaranteed prizes, urgency to act quickly.

- **How to Protect Yourself:** Legitimate lotteries and sweepstakes do not require you to pay fees to claim your prize. If someone asks for money to release your winnings, it's a scam.

Personal Information Scams

In personal information scams, the scammer asks for your personal details, such as your Social Security number, bank account information, or credit card number, supposedly to verify your identity or process your prize. This information is then used for identity theft or financial fraud.

- **Warning Signs:** Requests for sensitive personal information, threats of losing your prize if you don't provide the information.

- **How to Protect Yourself:** Never provide personal or financial information to unsolicited callers or emails. Verify the legitimacy of the prize independently.

Real-Life Lottery and Sweepstakes Scam Examples

Consider the story of Alice, who received a letter in the mail stating she had won a large sum of money in a foreign lottery. To claim her prize, she was instructed to wire a processing fee. Excited about her unexpected windfall, Alice sent the money, but she never received her prize. The letter was a scam, and Alice lost the money she sent.

Another example is John, who received a phone call from someone claiming to be from a well-known sweepstakes company. The caller said John had won a car, but to receive it, he needed to provide his Social Security number and bank details for verification. Trusting the caller, John provided the information, only to discover later that his identity had been stolen and his bank account drained.

How to Recognize Lottery and Sweepstakes Scams

Here are some key signs that a lottery or sweepstakes notification might be a scam:

- **Unexpected Winnings:** Be cautious if you receive a notification of winning a lottery or sweepstakes you didn't enter.

- **Upfront Fees:** Legitimate lotteries do not require you to pay fees to claim your prize.

- **Personal Information Requests:** Be wary of requests for sensitive information, such as your Social Security number or bank details.

- **Urgent Language:** Scammers often use urgency to pressure you into acting quickly without verifying the information.

Steps to Protect Yourself from Lottery and Sweepstakes Scams

- **Verify the Source:** If you receive a notification about winning a prize, verify the legitimacy of the organization independently. Look up their contact information and reach out to them directly.

- **Do Not Pay Fees:** Legitimate lotteries and sweepstakes do not ask for fees to claim prizes. If someone asks for money upfront, it's a scam.

- **Avoid Sharing Personal Information:** Do not provide personal or financial information to unsolicited callers or emails. Legitimate organizations will not ask for sensitive information in this manner.

- **Be Skeptical of Foreign Lotteries:** Most foreign lottery promotions are illegal in the U.S. If you receive a notification from a foreign lottery, it's likely a scam.

Reporting Lottery and Sweepstakes Scams

If you suspect a lottery or sweepstakes scam, it's important to report it. Here's how you can do it:

- **Federal Trade Commission (FTC):** File a complaint with the FTC at www.ftc.gov/com plaint.

- **United States Postal Inspection Service:** If the scam involves mail, report it to the Postal Inspection Service at www.uspis.gov.

- **State Attorney General's Office:** Contact your state's attorney general to report the scam and seek advice.

Additional Resources for Learning About Lottery and Sweepstakes Scams

- **FTC's Consumer Information:** Provides information on how to identify and report lottery and sweepstakes scams at https://consumer.ftc.gov/.

- **AARP Fraud Watch Network:** Offers resources and tips for recognizing and avoiding lottery and sweepstakes scams at https://www.aarp.org/money/scams-fraud/about-fraud-watch-network/.

- **Better Business Bureau (BBB):** Provides information on common scams and tips for protecting yourself at https://www.bbb.org/.

By staying vigilant and following these tips, you can protect yourself from lottery and sweepstakes scams and safeguard your personal information.

Remember, if it sounds too good to be true, it probably is.

Charity Scams

Charity scams exploit people's generosity and desire to help others, especially during times of crisis or disaster. Scammers pose as legitimate charitable organizations to solicit donations, which they then pocket for themselves. Understanding how these scams operate and recognizing their warning signs can help you ensure your contributions go to genuine causes.

How Charity Scams Work

In charity scams, fraudsters create fake charities or pose as representatives of real ones. They use emotional appeals and urgent language to solicit donations. These scams can occur through phone calls, emails, social media, or even in person. The goal is to steal your money and sometimes your personal information.

Fake Charities

Scammers set up fake charities that mimic real ones. They might create websites that look legitimate, use names similar to well-known organizations, and even have fake reviews or testimonials.

- **Warning Signs:** Unsolicited requests for donations, high-pressure tactics, lack of detailed information about the charity's mission or how funds are used.

- **How to Protect Yourself:** Research the charity independently before donating. Use websites like Charity Navigator or GuideStar to verify the legitimacy of the organization.

Impersonation of Real Charities

Scammers pose as representatives of well-known charities, contacting you through phone calls, emails, or social media. They use the reputation of these organizations to gain your trust and solicit donations.

- **Warning Signs:** Requests for donations via unusual methods (e.g., wire transfers, gift cards), misspellings or slight variations in the charity's name, reluctance to provide detailed information.

- **How to Protect Yourself:** Contact the charity directly using contact information from their official website to verify the request.

Real-Life Charity Scam Examples

Consider the story of Emily, who received a phone call from someone claiming to be from a well-known disaster relief organization. The caller used emotional language to describe the dire situation and urgently requested a donation. Emily, wanting to help, provided her credit card information over the phone. Later, she discovered unauthorized charges

on her account, and the caller turned out to be a
scammer.

Another example is Frank, who saw a social media
post from what appeared to be a legitimate charity
asking for donations to help children in need. The
post included heart-wrenching photos and stories.
Moved by the plea, Frank donated through the link
provided. It wasn't until later that he found out the
charity was fake, and his money had gone to the
scammer.

How to Recognize Charity Scams

Here are some key signs that a charitable request
might be a scam:

- **Unsolicited Requests:** Be cautious of unsolicited requests for donations, especially those that come through phone calls or
  emails.

- **High-Pressure Tactics:** Scammers often create a sense of urgency, pressuring you to

donate immediately.

- **Lack of Detailed Information:** Legitimate charities are transparent about their mission, how donations are used, and provide contact information.

- **Unusual Payment Methods:** Be wary if the charity requests donations via wire transfers, gift cards, or other unusual methods.

Steps to Protect Yourself from Charity Scams

Research the Charity: Before donating, research the charity independently. Use resources like Charity Navigator, GuideStar, or the Better Business Bureau's Wise Giving Alliance to verify the organization's legitimacy.

Ask Questions: Don't be afraid to ask detailed questions about the charity's mission, how donations are used, and the organization's history. Legitimate charities will be transparent and willing to provide information.

Donate Directly: Instead of donating through links provided in unsolicited messages, visit the charity's official website and donate directly through their secure donation page.

Beware of High-Pressure Tactics: Legitimate charities will not pressure you to donate immediately. Take your time to verify the request and make an informed decision.

Use Secure Payment Methods: Avoid donating via wire transfers or gift cards. Use credit cards or checks, which offer more security and the ability to dispute charges if necessary.

Reporting Charity Scams

If you suspect a charity scam, it's important to report it. Here's how you can do it:

- **Federal Trade Commission (FTC):** File a complaint with the FTC at www.ftc.gov/com plaint.

- **Better Business Bureau (BBB):** Report the scam to the BBB's Wise Giving Alliance at w ww.give.org.

- **State Attorney General's Office:** Contact your state's attorney general to report the scam and seek advice.

Additional Resources for Learning About Charity Scams

- **Charity Navigator:** Provides ratings and information on thousands of charitable organizations to help you make informed donation decisions at https://www.charitynavigator.org/.

- **GuideStar:** Offers detailed reports on non-profit organizations, including financial information and transparency ratings at https://www.guidestar.org/.

- **BBB Wise Giving Alliance:** Provides information on charities and evaluates them based on rigorous standards for accountability and transparency at www.give.org.

- **FTC's Consumer Information:** Offers tips and resources for recognizing and avoiding charity scams at https://consumer.ftc.gov/.

By staying vigilant and following these tips, you can protect yourself from charity scams and ensure your donations go to genuine causes. Remember, taking a little extra time to verify the legitimacy of a charity can make a big difference in making sure your generosity is not exploited.

Tech Support Scams

Tech support scams are designed to trick you into believing that your computer or device has a serious problem that requires immediate attention. Scammers pose as technical support representatives from well-known companies, using fear and urgency to manipulate you into giving them access to your device or paying for unnecessary services. Understanding these scams and how to recognize them can help you protect your personal information and your computer.

How Tech Support Scams Work

In tech support scams, fraudsters contact you through phone calls, pop-up messages, or emails, claiming to be from reputable tech companies like Microsoft, Apple, or your internet service provider. They might say that your computer is infected with a virus, that your personal information is at risk, or that there is some other urgent technical issue that needs immediate attention.

Phone Call Scams

In phone call scams, you receive an unsolicited call from someone claiming to be a tech support representative. They often use technical jargon to sound credible and may ask you to grant them remote access to your computer to "fix" the problem. Once they have access, they can install malware, steal your personal information, or charge you for fake services.

- **Warning Signs:** Unsolicited calls, urgent warnings about your computer, requests for remote access, demands for payment.

- **How to Protect Yourself:** Hang up and contact the company directly using a verified phone number. Legitimate tech companies do not make unsolicited phone calls offering support.

Pop-Up Message Scams

Pop-up message scams involve alarming pop-ups appearing on your computer screen, warning you about viruses or security issues. The pop-up includes a phone number to call for tech support. If you call, you are connected to a scammer who will try to convince you to grant remote access or pay for unnecessary services.

- **Warning Signs:** Sudden pop-ups with urgent messages, phone numbers to call for support, warnings that your personal information is at risk.

- **How to Protect Yourself:** Do not call the number provided. Close the pop-up and run a virus scan using your trusted antivirus software.

Email Scams

In email scams, you receive an email that appears to be from a reputable tech company, warning you about issues with your computer. The email might include a link to a fake website or a phone number to call for support. The goal is to trick you into providing personal information or paying for fake services.

- **Warning Signs:** Unsolicited emails, urgent language, links to unfamiliar websites, phone numbers for tech support.

- **How to Protect Yourself:** Do not click on links or call numbers in unsolicited emails. Contact the company directly using verified contact information.

Real-Life Tech Support Scam Examples

Consider the story of David, who received a phone call from someone claiming to be from Microsoft. The caller said that his computer had been infected with a serious virus and needed immediate attention. David, worried about his data, followed the caller's instructions and granted remote access to his computer. The scammer installed malware and stole his personal information, leading to significant financial loss.

Another example is Susan, who saw a pop-up message on her computer warning that her system was at risk and provided a phone number for immediate tech support. She called the number and was connected to a scammer who convinced her to pay for unnecessary services and software. Susan later discovered that her computer had no issues and that she had been scammed.

How to Recognize Tech Support Scams

Here are some key signs that a tech support offer might be a scam:

- **Unsolicited Contact:** Be wary of unsolicited phone calls, emails, or pop-ups claiming to be from tech support.

- **Urgent Language:** Scammers often use urgent language to create panic and prompt immediate action.

- **Requests for Remote Access:** Legitimate tech support will not ask for remote access to your computer unless you initiated the contact through verified channels.

- **Demands for Payment:** Be cautious if asked to pay for services upfront, especially if the request comes from an unsolicited source.

Steps to Protect Yourself from Tech Support Scams

- **Verify the Source:** If you receive an unsolicited tech support offer, contact the company directly using a known phone number or website.

- **Don't Grant Remote Access:** Never allow remote access to your computer unless you are certain you are dealing with a legitimate tech support representative.

- **Use Trusted Antivirus Software:** Keep your antivirus software updated and run regular scans to detect and remove malware.

- **Report Suspicious Activity:** Report any suspicious tech support offers to the relevant authorities and your tech company's support team.

Reporting Tech Support Scams

If you suspect a tech support scam, it's important to report it. Here's how you can do it:

- **Federal Trade Commission (FTC):** File a complaint with the FTC at www.ftc.gov/com

plaint.

- **Microsoft's Report a Scam:** If the scam involves someone pretending to be from Microsoft, report it at www.microsoft.com/rep ortascam.

- **Local Law Enforcement:** Contact your local police department to report the scam and seek advice.

Additional Resources for Learning About Tech Support Scams

- **FTC's Consumer Information:** Provides information on how to identify and report tech support scams at https://consumer.ftc.gov/.

- **Microsoft's Scam Information:** Offers tips and resources for recognizing and avoiding tech support scams at www.microsoft.com/ reportascam.

- **StaySafeOnline:** Offers resources and tips for recognizing and avoiding tech support scams at https://staysafeonline.org/.

By staying vigilant and following these tips, you can protect yourself from tech support scams and keep your personal information and computer safe. Remember, legitimate tech companies do not make unsolicited contact offering support, so always verify before taking any action.

Romance Scams

Romance scams exploit the emotions and trust of individuals looking for companionship or love online. Scammers create fake profiles on dating sites and social media platforms, building a relationship with their targets to eventually manipulate them into giving money or personal information. Understanding how these scams work and recognizing the warning signs can help protect your heart and wallet.

How Romance Scams Work

In romance scams, fraudsters create fake profiles using stolen photos and fictitious identities. They engage in conversations, building trust and emotional connections with their targets. Once a relationship is established, they fabricate stories to elicit sympathy and financial support.

Long-Distance Relationships

Scammers often claim to be living or working abroad, making it difficult to meet in person. They may use this distance as an excuse for why they can't meet face-to-face, but their true intention is to create a barrier that helps maintain the deception.

- **Warning Signs:** Requests for money to cover travel expenses, sudden emergencies requiring financial help, reluctance to meet in person.

- **How to Protect Yourself:** Be cautious of

long-distance relationships that involve frequent requests for money. Verify their identity through video calls and background checks.

Military Romance Scams

Scammers pose as military personnel stationed overseas. They use the respect and trust associated with the military to manipulate their targets, often claiming they need money for leave, medical expenses, or other urgent needs.

- **Warning Signs:** Requests for money to cover military expenses, claims of being in a dangerous or secretive location, reluctance to provide military ID or other verification.

- **How to Protect Yourself:** Verify their identity through official military channels. Be wary of requests for money from someone claiming to be in the military.

Widowed or Divorced Scams

Scammers may pose as widowed or divorced individuals, using their supposed past experiences to build a connection with their targets. They often claim to have children or family members who are also in need of financial assistance.

- **Warning Signs:** Heart-wrenching stories about past losses, requests for money to help children or other family members, overly dramatic or detailed personal stories.

- **How to Protect Yourself:** Be skeptical of overly dramatic stories. Verify their identity and the authenticity of their claims through independent sources.

Real-Life Romance Scam Examples

Consider the story of Carol, who met someone on a dating site who claimed to be a widowed engineer working on an oil rig. After months of daily communication, the scammer claimed to have an emergency and needed money to pay for equipment repairs. Trusting the relationship, Carol sent money several times, only to realize later that she had been scammed and the person she thought she knew didn't exist.

Another example is Robert, who began chatting with a woman on social media who claimed to be a nurse working overseas. After a few weeks, she asked for money to cover medical bills and travel expenses to visit him. Robert sent the money, but the woman disappeared, and he never heard from her again. The profile was fake, and Robert was left feeling betrayed and financially hurt.

How to Recognize Romance Scams

Here are some key signs that a romantic interest might be a scam:

- **Rapid Declarations of Love:** Be cautious if someone professes love or deep affection very quickly.

- **Requests for Money:** Scammers often ask

for money to cover travel expenses, medical bills, or other emergencies.

- **Avoiding Face-to-Face Meetings:** If someone makes excuses to avoid meeting in person or through video calls, it's a red flag.

- **Inconsistent Stories:** Pay attention to inconsistencies in their stories or personal details that don't add up.

Steps to Protect Yourself from Romance Scams

- **Verify Their Identity:** Use reverse image searches on their profile photos to check for stolen images. Ask for video calls to confirm their identity.

- **Be Skeptical of Requests for Money:** Never send money to someone you haven't met in person, regardless of how compelling their story might be.

- **Take Your Time:** Genuine relationships develop over time. Be wary of anyone who tries to rush the relationship or move too quickly.

- **Keep Personal Information Private:** Avoid sharing sensitive information like your home address, financial details, or social security number with someone you've met online.

- **Consult Friends or Family:** Discuss the relationship with trusted friends or family members. They can offer an outside perspective and help identify potential red flags.

Reporting Romance Scams

If you suspect a romance scam, it's important to report it. Here's how you can do it:

- **Federal Trade Commission (FTC):** File a complaint with the FTC at www.ftc.gov/complaint.

- **Dating Site or Social Media Platform:** Report the scam to the platform where you met the individual. Most sites have tools to report suspicious profiles and activity.

- **Local Law Enforcement:** Contact your local police department to report the scam and seek advice.

Additional Resources for Learning About Romance Scams

- **FTC's Consumer Information:** Provides information on how to identify and report romance scams at. https://consumer.ftc.gov/.

- **AARP Fraud Watch Network:** Offers resources and tips for recognizing and avoiding romance scams at https://www.aarp.org/money/scams-fraud/about-fraud-watch-network/.

- **Better Business Bureau (BBB):** Provides information on common scams and tips for protecting yourself at https://www.bbb.org/.

By staying vigilant and following these tips, you can protect yourself from romance scams and ensure that your online relationships are genuine. Remember, if something feels off, trust your instincts and take steps to verify the person's identity.

Home Repair Scams

Home repair scams take advantage of homeowners needing repairs or improvements. Scammers often offer services at a discount or claim to have materials left over from another job. Once paid, they either do substandard work or disappear without completing the job. Knowing how these scams operate and recognizing their warning signs can help you protect your home and your wallet.

How Home Repair Scams Work

In home repair scams, fraudsters pose as contractors or handymen, offering to perform repairs or improvements at a discounted rate. They often target vulnerable homeowners, such as the elderly, and use high-pressure sales tactics to secure quick agreements and payments.

Storm Chasers

Storm chasers are scammers who appear after severe weather events, offering to repair damage caused by storms. They claim to have materials left over from another job or offer a special deal because they're already working in the area.

- **Warning Signs:** Unsolicited offers for repairs, high-pressure tactics to sign contracts quickly, demands for upfront payments.

- **How to Protect Yourself:** Verify the contractor's credentials and check for local references. Avoid making hasty decisions under pressure.

Door-to-Door Contractors

Door-to-door contractors solicit work by knocking on your door and offering to perform repairs or improvements at a low cost. They may claim to notice a problem with your home that needs immediate attention.

- **Warning Signs:** Unsolicited offers, reluctance to provide written estimates or contracts, requests for cash payments.

- **How to Protect Yourself:** Get multiple estimates and verify the contractor's credentials. Insist on written contracts and avoid cash payments.

Lowball Estimates

Some scammers offer low estimates to secure the job and then demand more money once the work has begun, claiming unforeseen complications or additional necessary repairs.

- **Warning Signs:** Estimates significantly lower than others, vague or incomplete contracts, reluctance to provide detailed cost breakdowns.

- **How to Protect Yourself:** Get multiple estimates and compare them. Ensure the contract includes detailed descriptions of the
work to be done and the total cost.

Real-Life Home Repair Scam Examples

Consider the story of Betty, who was approached by
a contractor offering to fix her roof at a significant
discount, claiming he had leftover materials from a
nearby job. Betty paid him upfront, but the contractor never returned to complete the work. When she
tried to contact him, he was unreachable.

Another example is Tom, who hired a door-to-door
contractor to repave his driveway. The contractor
demanded a cash payment upfront and completed
only part of the job before disappearing. Tom was
left with an unfinished driveway and no way to recover his money.

How to Recognize Home Repair Scams

Here are some key signs that a home repair offer might be a scam:

- **Unsolicited Offers:** Be cautious of contractors who show up uninvited and offer their services.

- **High-Pressure Tactics:** Scammers often create a sense of urgency to prompt immediate decisions and payments.

- **Demands for Upfront Payments:** Legitimate contractors typically do not require full payment before starting the work.

- **Lack of Credentials:** Be wary of contractors who cannot provide proper identification, licensing, or insurance information.

Steps to Protect Yourself from Home Repair Scams

- **Verify Credentials:** Ask for proof of licensing, insurance, and bonding. Verify this information with local authorities or professional organizations.

- **Get Multiple Estimates:** Obtain written estimates from at least three different contractors to compare prices and services.

- **Check References:** Ask for and contact references from past clients. Research online reviews and ratings.

- **Insist on a Written Contract:** Ensure the contract includes detailed descriptions of the work to be done, the total cost, and a payment schedule. Avoid signing anything until you fully understand the terms.

- **Avoid Cash Payments:** Use checks or credit cards for payments, as these provide a record of the transaction and offer more protection in case of disputes.

Reporting Home Repair Scams

If you suspect a home repair scam, it's important to report it. Here's how you can do it:

- **Local Consumer Protection Office:** Contact your local consumer protection office or attorney general's office to report the scam.

- **Better Business Bureau (BBB):** File a complaint with the BBB at www.bbb.org.

- **Federal Trade Commission (FTC):** Report the scam to the FTC at www.ftc.gov/complaint.

- **Local Law Enforcement:** Contact your local police department to report the scam and seek advice.

Additional Resources for Learning About Home Repair Scams

- **Better Business Bureau (BBB):** Provides information on common scams and tips for finding reputable contractors at https://www.bbb.org/.

- **FTC's Consumer Information:** Offers tips and resources for recognizing and avoiding home repair scams at https://consumer.ftc.gov/.

- **AARP Fraud Watch Network:** Provides resources and tips specifically for seniors to avoid home repair scams at https://www.aarp.org/money/scams-fraud/about-fraud-watch-network/.

By staying vigilant and following these tips, you can protect yourself from home repair scams and ensure your home repairs and improvements are completed by reputable professionals. Remember, taking the time to verify credentials and compare estimates can save you from significant financial loss and frustration.

Three

Safe Practices

❤

Protecting yourself from scams and fraud requires adopting safe practices in your daily life. These practices help safeguard your personal information, secure your online activities, and build habits that reduce the risk of falling victim to scams. This chapter will provide practical tips and steps you can take to enhance your security.

In today's digital age, the threats posed by cybercriminals are ever-present. From phishing emails to identity theft, the tactics used by scammers are constantly evolving. However, by incorporating safe practices into your routine, you can significantly reduce your risk of falling victim to these schemes. It's important to remember that security is not a one-time effort but an ongoing process that requires vigilance and adaptability.

Why Safe Practices Matter

Adopting safe practices is crucial for several reasons:

- **Protection of Personal Information:** Your personal information is valuable. Scammers can use it to steal your identity, access your bank accounts, and commit fraud in your name.

- **Prevention of Financial Loss:** Falling victim to a scam can lead to significant financial losses. By staying informed and cautious, you can protect your hard-earned money.

- **Peace of Mind:** Knowing that you have taken steps to protect yourself can give you peace of mind. You can navigate the digital world with confidence, knowing that you are doing everything possible to stay safe.

- **Empowerment:** Being proactive about your security empowers you to take control of your digital life. You become less vulnerable to threats and better equipped to handle any suspicious activity.

The Scope of Safe Practices

This chapter will cover various aspects of safe practices, including:

- **Creating Strong Passwords:** How to create and manage passwords that are difficult for scammers to guess.

- **Two-Factor Authentication:** The benefits of adding an extra layer of security to your accounts.

- **Recognizing Secure Websites:** Tips for ensuring that the websites you visit and shop on are secure.

- **Safe Browsing Tips:** Best practices for browsing the internet safely and avoiding malicious sites.

- **Verifying Caller Identity:** How to handle unsolicited phone calls and verify the identity of the caller.

- **Recognizing Red Flags:** Common warning signs of scams and how to respond to them.

- **Keeping Personal Information Private:** Strategies for safeguarding your personal information online and offline.

- **Staying Informed:** The importance of staying updated on new scams and threats.

By following the guidelines and tips provided in this chapter, you can create a safer environment for yourself both online and offline. Remember, staying safe is an ongoing effort that requires awareness and proactive measures.

***

Creating Strong Passwords

Strong passwords are your first line of defense against unauthorized access to your accounts. Using weak or easily guessable passwords makes it easier for scammers to gain access to your personal information. In today's digital world, where many of our activities and transactions occur online, having robust passwords is essential for maintaining your security.

Tips for Creating Strong Passwords

1. **Use a Mix of Characters:**

   - Combine uppercase and lowercase letters, numbers, and special characters.

   - Example: Instead of "password," use "P@sshssw0rd1!6753"

2. **Avoid Common Words and Phrases:**

   - Avoid using easily guessable information

like birthdays, names, or common words.

- Example: Instead of "JohnDoe123," use "Jd@94$*!z111232"

3. **Make It Long:**

- Aim for a password that is at least 12 characters long. Longer passwords are harder to crack.

- Example: "E8@r&L4o9z!M7h"

4. **Use Unique Passwords for Each Account:**

- Avoid reusing passwords across multiple accounts. Each account should have its own unique password to prevent a breach in one account from compromising others.

- Example: Your email password should be different from your online banking password.

Examples of Strong vs. Weak Passwords

- **Weak Password:** Password123

- **Strong Password:** 7g&$L9x!B@q1Y

Weak passwords are often simple and easy to remember, but they are also easy for scammers to guess. Strong passwords, on the other hand, are complex and unique, making them much more difficult for unauthorized users to crack.

Tools for Managing Passwords

Password Managers: Consider using a password manager to generate and store strong passwords. Password managers can securely store all your passwords, so you only need to remember one master password. They can also help you create complex passwords for new accounts.

Recommendations for Reliable Password Managers

- **LastPass:** A popular password manager that offers both free and premium versions. It provides secure storage for passwords and other sensitive information.

- **1Password:** Known for its user-friendly interface and robust security features. It allows you to store passwords, credit card information, and secure notes.

- **Dashlane:** Offers comprehensive security tools and a free trial period. Dashlane includes a password generator and dark web monitoring to alert you if your information is compromised.

Additional Tips for Password Security

- **Regularly Update Your Passwords:** Change your passwords regularly to reduce the risk of unauthorized access. Aim to update critical account passwords, such as banking and email, every few months.

- **Avoid Writing Down Passwords:** Do not

write down your passwords where they can be easily found. If you must write them down, store them in a secure location.

- **Enable Two-Factor Authentication (2FA):** Whenever possible, enable two-factor authentication for an added layer of security. This requires you to provide a second form of verification, such as a code sent to your phone, in addition to your password.

By following these guidelines, you can create strong, secure passwords that protect your personal information and online accounts from scammers. Remember, your password is your first line of defense—make it a strong one.

Two-Factor Authentication

Two-Factor Authentication (2FA) adds an extra layer of security to your online accounts. Even if someone manages to get hold of your password, they would still need the second factor to gain access. This significantly reduces the chances of unauthorized access and helps protect your personal information.

What is Two-Factor Authentication?

Two-Factor Authentication requires two forms of identification before granting access to an account:

- **Something You Know:** Your password.

- **Something You Have:** A secondary form of verification, such as a code sent to your phone, an authentication app, or a physical security key.

Benefits of Two-Factor Authentication

- **Enhanced Security:** Adds an extra layer of defense against unauthorized access.

- **Reduces Risk of Identity Theft:** Makes it

harder for scammers to access your accounts, even if they have your password.

- **Protects Sensitive Information:** Helps safeguard your financial and personal data.

Types of Two-Factor Authentication

- **SMS-Based 2FA:**

  - A code is sent to your mobile phone via text message.

  - Example: After entering your password, you receive a text with a code that you must enter to gain access.

- **App-Based 2FA:**

  - An authentication app generates a time-based code.

  - Example: Apps like Google Authenticator or Authy provide a code that changes every 30 seconds.

- **Email-Based 2FA:**

  - A code is sent to your registered email address.

  - Example: After entering your password, you receive an email with a verification code.

- **Physical Security Keys:**

  - A USB or NFC device that you plug into your computer or tap on your phone.

  - Example: YubiKey or Google Titan Security Key.

How to Set Up Two-Factor Authentication

- **Choose Your Method:**

  - Decide which form of 2FA you prefer (SMS, app-based, email, or physical security key).

- **Enable 2FA on Your Accounts:**

  - Most online services offer 2FA in their security settings. Look for options like "Security" or "Login Settings."

- Follow the prompts to set up 2FA. You may need to provide your phone number, download an authentication app, or register a security key.

- **Follow the Setup Instructions:**

  - Enter the required information and complete the verification process. This usually involves receiving and entering a code or connecting a security key.

- **Store Backup Codes:**

  - Some services provide backup codes in case you lose access to your 2FA method (e.g., losing your phone). Store these codes securely.

Popular Services Offering Two-Factor Authentication

- **Google:** Enable 2FA through your Google ac-

count settings using SMS, Google Authenticator, or a security key.

- **Facebook:** Enable 2FA through Facebook's
  security settings using SMS or an authentication app.

- **Apple:** Enable 2FA for your Apple ID using
  SMS or a trusted device.

- **Banks and Financial Institutions:** Most
  banks offer 2FA for online banking. Check
  your bank's website or app for setup instructions.

Additional Tips for Using Two-Factor Authentication

- **Use Different Methods for Different Accounts:** If possible, use different 2FA methods for different accounts to enhance security.

- **Keep Your Phone Secure:** If you use
  SMS-based 2FA, ensure your phone is secure

and not easily accessible to others.

- **Regularly Update Your Contact Information:** Ensure that your phone number and email address are up to date in your account settings.

By enabling Two-Factor Authentication, you add a robust layer of security to your online accounts, significantly reducing the risk of unauthorized access. Remember, 2FA is one of the most effective ways to protect your personal information online.

Recognizing Secure Websites

When browsing the internet, especially when entering personal information or making online purchases, it's crucial to ensure that the websites you visit are secure. Secure websites protect your data from being intercepted by scammers and provide a safer online experience.

How to Recognize Secure Websites

- **Look for "https://" in the URL**

  - Secure websites use "https://" rather than "http://". The "s" stands for "secure" and indicates that the website uses encryption to protect your data.

  - Example: "https://www.yourbank.com" is secure, while "http://www.yourbank.com" is not.

- **Check for a Padlock Icon**

  - A padlock icon in the address bar indicates that the website uses a secure connection. Clicking on the padlock provides more information about the security certificate.

  - Example: In most browsers, you'll see a padlock icon to the left of the URL.

- **Verify the Website's Security Certificate**

  - Clicking on the padlock icon allows you to

view the website's security certificate. Ensure that the certificate is valid and issued by a trusted authority.

- ○ Example: A valid certificate will show details like the issuing authority and the website's identity.

- **Check the URL for Misspellings**

  - ○ Scammers often create fake websites with URLs that look similar to legitimate sites. Double-check the URL for misspellings or unusual characters.

  - ○ Example: "yourbank.com" is legitimate, but "yourbannk.com" could be a scam.

- **Use Browser Security Features**

  - ○ Modern web browsers have built-in security features that warn you about potentially dangerous websites. Pay attention to these warnings and avoid sites flagged as unsafe.

  - ○ Example: Browsers like Chrome, Firefox, and Edge will display warnings if a site is suspected of phishing or contains malware.

Tips for Safe Online Shopping

- **Shop on Reputable Websites**

  - Stick to well-known and trusted online retailers. If you're unsure about a website, search for reviews and check its reputation before making a purchase.

  - Example: Use sites like Amazon, eBay, or well-known brand websites.

- **Avoid Public Wi-Fi for Transactions**

  - Avoid making online purchases or entering sensitive information when connected to public Wi-Fi networks. These networks are often less secure and can be targeted by hackers.

  - Example: Wait until you're on a secure, private network at home.

- **Use Secure Payment Methods**

  - Use credit cards or secure payment services like PayPal for online transactions. These methods offer better protection and dispute resolution compared to debit cards or bank transfers.

  - Example: PayPal offers buyer protection that can help resolve disputes with sellers.

- **Be Cautious with Pop-Up Ads**

  - Avoid clicking on pop-up ads or offers that seem too good to be true. These can lead to malicious websites or phishing attempts.

  - Example: If you see an ad offering a high-value item at an extremely low price, it's likely a scam.

Protecting Your Personal Information

- **Limit the Information You Share**

- Only provide the necessary information when creating accounts or making purchases online. Be cautious about sharing personal details like your social security number or birthdate.

- Example: Most online stores only need your name, address, and payment information.

- **Enable Two-Factor Authentication (2FA)**

- Enable 2FA on accounts that offer it, especially for online banking and shopping sites. This adds an extra layer of security.

- Example: Many online retailers and financial institutions offer 2FA as an additional security measure.

- **Monitor Your Accounts Regularly**

- Regularly check your bank and credit card statements for unauthorized transactions. Report any suspicious activity immediately.

- Example: Set up alerts with your bank to

notify you of large or unusual transactions.

Additional Resources for Recognizing Secure Websites

- **StaySafeOnline:** Offers resources and tips for safe browsing and recognizing secure websites at https://staysafeonline.org/.

- **Federal Trade Commission (FTC):** Provides information on safe online shopping and avoiding scams at https://consumer.ftc.gov/.

- **Better Business Bureau (BBB):** Offers tips for finding reputable online retailers and avoiding fraudulent websites at https://www.bbb.org/.

By following these guidelines, you can ensure that the websites you visit are secure and that your personal information is protected. Always take a moment to verify the security of a website before entering any sensitive information.

***

Safe Browsing Tips

Browsing the internet safely is crucial to protecting your personal information and avoiding scams. Unsafe browsing habits can lead to malware infections, phishing attacks, and data breaches. By following safe browsing practices, you can reduce your risk and enjoy a more secure online experience.

Tips for Safe Browsing

- **Keep Your Browser Updated**

  - Regularly update your web browser to ensure you have the latest security features and patches.

  - Example: Enable automatic updates for your browser to stay protected against new threats.

- **Use a Secure Browser**

  - Choose browsers known for their security features, such as Google Chrome, Mozilla Firefox, or Microsoft Edge.

  - Example: These browsers offer built-in protection against phishing and malware.

- **Enable Pop-Up Blockers**

  - Pop-up ads can be annoying and sometimes malicious. Use your browser's pop-up blocker to prevent them from appearing.

  - Example: Most browsers have a pop-up blocker feature that you can enable in the settings.

- **Avoid Clicking on Suspicious Links**

  - Be cautious of links in emails, social media posts, and websites that seem suspicious. Hover over the link to see where it leads before clicking.

  - Example: If a link looks strange or comes from an unknown source, don't click on it.

- **Use Bookmarks for Frequent Sites**

  - Bookmark the websites you visit frequently to avoid mistyping URLs and accidentally visiting malicious sites.

  - Example: Create bookmarks for your bank, email provider, and other frequently visited sites.

- **Be Wary of Free Downloads**

  - Free downloads can sometimes come bundled with malware. Only download software from trusted sources.

  - Example: Avoid downloading software from unknown websites or through pop-up ads.

- **Read Privacy Policies**

  - Before entering personal information on a website, read its privacy policy to understand how your data will be used and protected.

  - Example: Look for clear explanations of data usage and whether your information will be shared with third parties.

Using Security Software

- **Install Antivirus Software**

  - Use reputable antivirus software to protect your computer from malware and other threats.

  - Example: Programs like Norton, McAfee, and Bitdefender offer comprehensive protection.

- **Enable Firewall Protection**

  - A firewall helps block unauthorized access to your computer. Ensure your firewall is enabled and configured correctly.

  - Example: Both Windows and macOS have built-in firewall features that you can activate.

- **Use a Virtual Private Network (VPN)**

- A VPN encrypts your internet connection, providing additional privacy and security, especially on public Wi-Fi.

- Example: Services like Proton VPN, Nord-VPN, ExpressVPN, and CyberGhost offer reliable VPN options.

Recognizing Phishing Attempts

- **Check the Sender's Email Address**

  - Verify that the email address is legitimate and not a slight variation of a trusted source.

  - Example: "support@paypal.com" is legitimate, but "support@paaypal.com" is a scam.

- **Look for Misspellings and Grammar Errors**

  - Scammers often make mistakes in their messages. Be cautious of emails with poor spelling and grammar.

- Example: "Your account has been compromized" instead of "compromised."

- **Beware of Urgent Requests**

  - Phishing emails often create a sense of urgency to prompt immediate action. Be skeptical of urgent requests for personal information or payments.

  - Example: An email stating "Your account will be locked in 24 hours if you don't update your password" is likely a scam.

Staying Informed

- **Stay Updated on New Scams**

  - Keep yourself informed about the latest scams and threats by following reputable security blogs and websites.

  - Example: Websites like Krebs on Security – https://krebsonsecurity.com/ , StaySafeOnline – https://staysafeonline .org/, and the FTC's Scam Alerts – https

://consumer.ftc.gov/consumer-alerts offer valuable information.

- **Educate Yourself and Others**

  - Share what you've learned with friends and family to help them stay safe online.

  - Example: Discuss safe browsing tips with your loved ones and encourage them to adopt these practices.

Additional Resources for Safe Browsing

- **StaySafeOnline:** Offers resources and tips for safe internet browsing at https://staysafeonline.org/.

- **Federal Trade Commission (FTC):** Provides information on online safety and avoiding scams at https://consumer.ftc.gov/consumer-alerts.

- **Consumer Reports:** Offers reviews and recommendations for security software and tools at https://www.consumerreports.org/.

By following these safe browsing tips, you can protect yourself from online threats and ensure a safer, more secure internet experience. Remember, staying vigilant and cautious is key to maintaining your online security.

***

Verifying Caller Identity

With the rise of phone scams, it's crucial to verify the identity of callers, especially when they ask for personal information or money. Scammers often pose as legitimate organizations or individuals to gain your trust and exploit it. By learning how to verify caller identity, you can protect yourself from falling victim to these scams.

Tips for Verifying Caller Identity

- **Ask for Verification**

- If you receive a call from someone claiming to be from a legitimate organization, ask for their name, department, and a callback number. Then, verify the information by calling the organization directly using a known phone number.

- Example: If someone claims to be from your bank, call the bank's official customer service number to verify the call.

- **Don't Trust Caller ID**

  - Scammers can use technology to spoof caller ID, making it look like the call is coming from a legitimate source. Don't rely solely on caller ID to verify a caller's identity.

  - Example: A scammer might spoof a caller ID to display "IRS" or "Police" to trick you into answering the call.

- **Verify Through Official Channels**

  - Use official channels to verify the caller's identity. Look up the organization's contact information on their official website or a trusted directory.

- Example: If a caller claims to be from a government agency, visit the agency's official website and use the contact information provided there to verify the call.

- **Be Cautious with Unsolicited Calls**

  - Be wary of unsolicited calls, especially those asking for personal information or payments. Legitimate organizations typically do not ask for sensitive information over the phone.

  - Example: If you receive an unsolicited call from someone claiming to be from your credit card company, hang up and call the customer service number on the back of your card.

Common Caller ID Spoofing Scams

- **IRS Impersonation Scams**

  - Scammers pose as IRS agents, claiming you

owe taxes and must pay immediately to avoid arrest. They often use caller ID spoofing to display "IRS" or a similar name.

- How to Protect Yourself: The IRS will never call to demand immediate payment or ask for personal information over the phone. Verify by contacting the IRS directly.

- **Tech Support Scams**

  - Scammers call claiming to be from a well-known tech company, stating there's a problem with your computer that needs immediate attention. They use caller ID spoofing to display the company's name.

  - How to Protect Yourself: Legitimate tech companies do not make unsolicited calls. Verify by contacting the company directly through their official support channels.

- **Bank Scams**

  - Scammers pose as bank representatives, claiming there's an issue with your account and requesting personal information to resolve it. They use caller ID spoofing to display the bank's name.

- How to Protect Yourself: Banks typically do not ask for sensitive information over the phone. Verify by calling the bank's official customer service number.

Steps to Take if You Suspect a Scam Call

- **Hang Up Immediately**

  - If you suspect a call is a scam, hang up immediately. Do not engage with the caller or provide any personal information.

  - Example: If a caller demands immediate payment or personal information, hang up and verify through official channels.

- **Report the Call**

  - Report the suspicious call to the appropriate authorities, such as the Federal Trade Commission (FTC) or your local law enforcement.

- ◦ Example: File a complaint with the FTC at www.ftc.gov/complaint.

- **Block the Number**

  - ◦ Use your phone's call-blocking feature to block the number from which the suspicious call originated.

  - ◦ Example: Most smartphones have a call-blocking feature that you can access through the call history or settings.

Additional Tips for Phone Safety

- **Register with the National Do Not Call Registry**

  - ◦ Register your phone number with the National Do Not Call Registry to reduce the number of unsolicited calls you receive.

  - ◦ Example: Visit www.donotcall.gov to register your number.

- **Use Call-Blocking Apps**

- Consider using call-blocking apps or services to screen and block unwanted calls.

- Example: Apps like Verizon Call Filter, Hiya, Truecaller, and Nomorobo can help identify and block scam calls.

- **Educate Yourself and Others**

  - Stay informed about the latest phone scams and share this information with friends and family to help them stay safe.

  - Example: Discuss common phone scams with your loved ones and encourage them to verify caller identities.

Additional Resources for Verifying Caller Identity

- **Federal Trade Commission (FTC):** Provides information on phone scams and how to report them at https://consumer.ftc.gov/scams.

- **Federal Communications Commission**

(FCC): Offers tips for avoiding spoofing scams and protecting your phone number at https://www.fcc.gov/general/frauds-scams-and-alerts-guides.

- **AARP Fraud Watch Network:** Provides resources and tips specifically for seniors to avoid phone scams at https://www.aarp.org/money/scams-fraud/about-fraud-watch-network/.

By following these tips and verifying the identity of callers, you can protect yourself from phone scams and ensure that you only provide personal information to legitimate sources. Remember, it's always better to be cautious and take the time to verify than to risk falling victim to a scam.

Recognizing Red Flags

Scammers often use psychological tactics to create a sense of urgency, fear, or excitement, making it easier for them to deceive their victims. Recognizing the red flags of potential scams can help you stay alert and avoid falling into their traps. This section will highlight common warning signs and provide tips on how to respond to them.

Common Red Flags of Scams

- **Urgency and Pressure**

  - Scammers create a sense of urgency to pressure you into making quick decisions without thinking them through.

  - **Example:** "You must act now or you'll lose this opportunity!" or "Your account will be suspended if you don't respond immediately."

- **Requests for Personal Information**

  - Legitimate organizations rarely ask for sensitive information like Social Security numbers, bank account details, or passwords over the phone or via email.

- **Example:** "Please provide your Social Security number to verify your identity."

- **Unsolicited Offers or Prizes**

  - Be cautious of unsolicited messages or calls claiming that you have won a prize or offer that you did not apply for.

  - **Example:** "Congratulations! You've won a free vacation. Just pay the processing fee to claim your prize."

- **Too Good to Be True**

  - Offers that seem too good to be true often are. Scammers lure you with promises of easy money or high returns with little effort.

  - **Example:** "Invest $100 today and make $1,000 by the end of the week!"

- **Unusual Payment Methods**

  - Scammers often request payments via unconventional methods, such as gift cards, wire transfers, or cryptocurrencies.

- **Example:** "Please send payment via gift cards or wire transfer only."

- **Emotional Manipulation**

  - Scammers use emotional appeals to manipulate you into making decisions based on feelings rather than logic.

  - **Example:** "I'm in urgent need of help, and you're the only one I can trust."

How to Respond to Red Flags

- **Pause and Reflect**

  - Take a moment to think before reacting to urgent requests. Scammers rely on creating panic to prompt immediate action.

  - **Tip:** If something feels off, trust your instincts and take time to verify the situation.

- **Verify the Source**

- Independently verify the legitimacy of the request by contacting the organization directly using known contact information.

- **Tip:** Look up the official contact information and reach out to the organization to confirm the request.

- **Do Not Provide Personal Information**

  - Avoid sharing sensitive information unless you are certain of the request's legitimacy.

  - **Tip:** Legitimate organizations will not ask for personal information through unsolicited calls or emails.

- **Use Secure Payment Methods**

  - Only use secure and traceable payment methods when conducting transactions.

  - **Tip:** Credit cards offer more protection against fraud than gift cards or wire transfers.

- **Educate Yourself and Stay Informed**

  - Stay updated on common scams and red

flags by following reputable security blogs and resources.

- **Tip:** Knowledge is your best defense against scams. Share what you learn with friends and family to help them stay safe.

Real-Life Examples of Red Flags

- **Phishing Email Example**

  - Sarah received an email claiming to be from her bank, stating that her account had been compromised and she needed to verify her information immediately. The email included a link to a website that looked like her bank's login page. However, the email contained grammatical errors, and the link led to a suspicious URL. Sarah recognized these red flags and contacted her bank directly, confirming that the email was a phishing attempt.

- **Phone Scam Example**

○ John received a call from someone claiming to be an IRS agent, stating that he owed back taxes and would be arrested if he didn't pay immediately. The caller demanded payment via gift cards. John knew that the IRS would never request payment in this manner and hung up the phone. He reported the scam to the Federal Trade Commission (FTC).

Reporting Scams

If you encounter a scam, it's important to report it to the appropriate authorities. Here's how you can do it:

- **Federal Trade Commission (FTC):** File a complaint with the FTC at www.ftc.gov/complaint.

- **Better Business Bureau (BBB):** Report scams to the BBB at www.bbb.org/scamtracker.

- **State Attorney General's Office:** Contact

your state's attorney general to report scams and seek advice.

Additional Resources for Recognizing Red Flags

- **Federal Trade Commission (FTC):** Offers information on common scams and how to report them at www.ftc.gov/complaint.

- **Better Business Bureau (BBB):** Provides tips for recognizing scams and reporting fraudulent activity at www.bbb.org/scamtra cker.

- **StaySafeOnline:** Offers resources and tips for identifying and avoiding scams at https ://staysafeonline.org/.

By staying vigilant and recognizing red flags, you can protect yourself from scams and ensure your personal information and finances remain secure. Remember, when in doubt, take the time to verify and trust your instincts.

***

Keeping Personal Information Private

In today's digital age, safeguarding your personal information is more crucial than ever. Scammers and cybercriminals constantly seek ways to steal your identity, access your financial accounts, and commit fraud. By keeping your personal information private, you can significantly reduce the risk of these threats.

Tips for Keeping Personal Information Private

- **Be Selective About What You Share Online**
  - Avoid posting sensitive information on social media or other public platforms. Information like your full name, address, phone number, and birthdate can be used by scammers to steal your identity.

- **Example:** Instead of sharing your full birth-date on Facebook, consider only sharing the month and day.

- **Use Privacy Settings on Social Media**

  - Adjust the privacy settings on your social media accounts to control who can see your information and posts. Limit access to your profile to friends and family only.

  - **Example:** On Facebook, you can set your profile to "Friends Only" to restrict visibility to people you trust.

- **Avoid Oversharing in Emails and Messages**

  - Be cautious when sharing personal information via email or messaging apps. Ensure the recipient is trustworthy and that the platform is secure.

  - **Example:** Avoid sending your Social Security number or credit card details through email.

- **Shred Sensitive Documents**

- Shred documents containing personal information before disposing of them. This includes bank statements, medical records, and bills.

- **Example:** Use a cross-cut shredder to destroy old credit card statements and insurance documents.

- **Secure Your Devices**

  - Use strong passwords, biometric locks (fingerprint or facial recognition), and encryption to protect your devices. Enable automatic locking and remote wipe features.

  - **Example:** Set a strong password and enable fingerprint unlock on your smartphone.

- **Be Cautious with Public Wi-Fi**

  - Avoid accessing sensitive accounts or entering personal information when connected to public Wi-Fi networks. Use a Virtual Private Network (VPN) for added security.

- **Example:** Wait until you are on a secure, private network to check your bank account or make online purchases.

Protecting Your Financial Information

- **Monitor Your Accounts Regularly**

  - Regularly check your bank and credit card statements for unauthorized transactions. Report any suspicious activity immediately.

  - **Example:** Set up account alerts with your bank to notify you of large or unusual transactions.

- **Use Credit Monitoring Services**

  - Consider using credit monitoring services to keep an eye on your credit report and receive alerts for any unusual activity.

  - **Example:** Services like Experian, TransUnion, or Equifax offer credit monitoring and identity theft protection.

- **Be Careful with Online Shopping**

    - Only shop on secure websites and use secure payment methods. Avoid saving your payment information on websites whenever possible.

    - **Example:** Look for "https://" and a padlock icon in the URL bar before entering your payment details.

- **Beware of Phishing Scams**

    - Be cautious of unsolicited emails, texts, or calls asking for your personal or financial information. Verify the source before providing any details.

    - **Example:** If you receive an email from your bank asking for personal information, contact the bank directly using a known phone number.

Protecting Your Personal Information Offline

- **Secure Your Mailbox**

- Use a locked mailbox or a P.O. box to receive mail. Promptly collect your mail to prevent thieves from stealing sensitive information.

- **Example:** Consider a mailbox with a lock to protect your mail from theft.

- **Limit What You Carry**

  - Avoid carrying unnecessary personal information in your wallet or purse. Only carry essential items, such as your ID and a few payment cards.

  - **Example:** Leave your Social Security card and extra credit cards at home unless you need them.

- **Be Cautious with Personal Conversations**

  - Be mindful of where you discuss personal information. Avoid sharing sensitive details in public places where others can overhear.

  - **Example:** If you need to discuss financial matters, do so in a private setting.

Reporting Identity Theft and Fraud

If you suspect that your personal information has been compromised, take immediate action:

- **Contact Your Financial Institutions**

  - Notify your bank, credit card companies, and other financial institutions of any suspicious activity. They can help secure your accounts and prevent further fraud.

  - **Example:** Report unauthorized transactions to your bank and request a freeze on your accounts if necessary.

- **Place a Fraud Alert on Your Credit Report**

  - Contact the three major credit bureaus (Equifax, Experian, TransUnion) to place a fraud alert on your credit report. This makes it harder for scammers to open new accounts in your name.

  - **Example:** A fraud alert notifies potential creditors to verify your identity before extending credit.

- **File a Report with the Federal Trade Commission (FTC)**

  - The FTC provides resources and a recovery plan for identity theft victims. File a report at www.identitytheft.gov.

  - **Example:** Use the FTC's identity theft recovery plan to guide you through the steps to restore your identity.

Additional Resources for Keeping Personal Information Private

- **Federal Trade Commission (FTC):** Offers information on protecting your privacy and recovering from identity theft at https://consumer.ftc.gov/scams.

- **IdentityTheft.gov:** Provides a comprehensive recovery plan for identity theft victims at www.identitytheft.gov.

- **Better Business Bureau (BBB):** Offers tips

for protecting your personal information and avoiding scams at https://www.bbb.org/.

By following these tips and being vigilant about your privacy, you can protect your personal information from scammers and cybercriminals. Remember, safeguarding your information requires ongoing effort and awareness.

Staying Informed

Scammers and cybercriminals continuously adapt their tactics, making it essential to stay informed about the latest threats. By keeping up-to-date with current scams and fraud trends, you can better protect yourself and your loved ones. Staying informed also empowers you to recognize and respond to new threats effectively.

Ways to Stay Informed

- **Follow Reputable Security Blogs and Websites**

  - Security blogs and websites offer updates on the latest scams, cybersecurity tips, and advice on how to protect yourself.

  - **Example:** Websites like Krebs on Security, StaySafeOnline, and the Federal Trade Commission (FTC) provide valuable information.

- **Sign Up for Alerts and Newsletters**

  - Subscribe to newsletters and alerts from trusted sources to receive regular updates on new scams and cybersecurity threats.

  - **Example:** The FTC and AARP Fraud Watch Network offer email alerts about the latest scams and fraud prevention tips.

- **Join Community Groups and Forums**

  - Participate in online forums and community groups focused on cybersecurity and scam prevention. These groups can be a valuable source of information and support.

- ○ **Example:** Join groups on social media platforms like Facebook that focus on scam awareness and prevention.

- **Attend Webinars and Workshops**

  - ○ Many organizations offer free webinars and workshops on cybersecurity and scam prevention. Attending these events can enhance your knowledge and skills.

  - ○ **Example:** Local libraries, community centers, and online platforms like Eventbrite often host educational events.

- **Stay Updated on Software and Security Patches**

  - ○ Regularly update your devices, software, and security programs to protect against the latest vulnerabilities and threats.

  - ○ **Example:** Enable automatic updates for your operating system, antivirus software, and web browsers.

Sharing Information with Others

- **Educate Family and Friends**

  - Share what you've learned about scams and cybersecurity with your family and friends. Encourage them to stay informed and adopt safe practices.

  - **Example:** Discuss recent scam alerts at family gatherings or through group messages to keep everyone aware and vigilant.

- **Use Social Media Responsibly**

  - Share reliable information about scams and cybersecurity on your social media profiles. However, ensure the sources are credible before sharing.

  - **Example:** Post links to articles from reputable sources like the FTC or cybersecurity blogs to inform your network.

- **Organize Community Events**

- ○ Work with local organizations to organize community events focused on scam awareness and prevention. These events can help spread important information and build a supportive network.

- ○ **Example:** Collaborate with local senior centers to host a scam prevention workshop.

Recognizing Reliable Sources

- **Verify the Source's Credibility**

  - ○ Ensure that the information you receive comes from reputable and established sources. Avoid relying on unverified or sensationalist websites.

  - ○ **Example:** Trust information from government websites, well-known cybersecurity companies, and established news organizations.

- **Cross-Check Information**

- Cross-check information from multiple sources to verify its accuracy. Scammers often spread misinformation to create confusion.

- **Example:** If you read about a new scam, look for additional reports from other reputable sources before taking action.

- **Be Skeptical of Sensationalist Headlines**

  - Be cautious of headlines that seem overly sensational or designed to provoke fear. Scammers and unreliable sources often use such tactics to grab attention.

  - **Example:** Headlines that promise "exclusive" or "secret" ways to avoid scams should be verified through reputable sources.

Using Technology to Stay Informed

- **Install Security Software**

  - Use security software that provides

real-time alerts and updates on new threats. This software can help you stay informed and protect your devices.

- **Example:** Antivirus programs like Norton, McAfee, and Bitdefender offer features that keep you updated on the latest threats.

- **Enable Browser Security Features**

  - Modern browsers have security features that warn you about unsafe websites and phishing attempts. Enable these features to enhance your online safety.

  - **Example:** Use the built-in security features in browsers like Chrome, Firefox, and Edge to receive warnings about malicious sites.

- **Leverage Smart Devices**

  - Use smart devices, like home assistants, that can provide updates on security news and alerts.

  - **Example:** Ask your smart home device, such as Amazon Echo or Google Home, to provide the latest news on cybersecurity and scams.

Reporting Scams and Suspicious Activity

- **Report to Authorities**

  - Report scams and suspicious activity to relevant authorities, such as the FTC, local law enforcement, and consumer protection agencies.

  - **Example:** Use the FTC's online complaint form to report scams and help authorities track and combat fraud.

- **Share Your Experience**

  - Sharing your experience with scams can help others recognize and avoid similar threats. Use community platforms and forums to discuss your encounters.

  - **Example:** Post your scam experiences on community forums to alert others and provide tips on how to avoid similar situations.

Additional Resources for Staying Informed

- **Federal Trade Commission (FTC):** Provides regular updates on scams, cybersecurity tips, and consumer protection advice at https://consumer.ftc.gov/scams.

- **AARP Fraud Watch Network:** Offers resources and alerts specifically designed for seniors to stay informed about the latest scams at https://www.aarp.org/money/scams-fraud/about-fraud-watch-network/.

- **StaySafeOnline:** A platform dedicated to providing information on online safety and cybersecurity best practices at https://staysafeonline.org/.

By staying informed and sharing your knowledge with others, you can help create a safer environment for yourself and your community. Remember, staying updated on the latest threats is a continuous effort that can significantly enhance your security.

Four

Tools and Resources

In the fight against scams and fraud, having the right tools and resources at your disposal is essential. These tools can help you protect your personal information, secure your devices, and navigate the online world safely. As scammers become more sophisticated, utilizing these tools can provide an additional layer of defense, making it significantly harder for malicious actors to succeed.

Why Tools and Resources Matter

Every day, we rely more heavily on technology for communication, banking, shopping, and even healthcare. This increased reliance on digital solutions comes with its own set of risks. Cybercriminals continuously evolve their tactics to exploit vulnerabilities, whether through phishing attempts, malware infections, or data breaches. By equipping yourself with the right tools and resources, you can take proactive steps to mitigate these risks and protect yourself from potential threats.

Scope of This Chapter

This chapter will cover a range of tools and resources that can enhance your security and provide you with peace of mind, including:

- **Antivirus and Antimalware Software:** Protecting your devices from malicious software.

- **Password Managers:** Creating and managing strong, unique passwords for all your accounts.

- **Privacy Settings:** Adjusting settings on your devices and online accounts to maximize privacy.

- **Secure Browsing Tools:** Ensuring safe browsing practices and protecting your online activities.

- **Encryption Tools:** Safeguarding your data through encryption.

- **Two-Factor Authentication (2FA) Apps:** Adding an extra layer of security to your accounts.

- **Educational Resources:** Staying informed about the latest scams and cybersecurity best practices.

How These Tools and Resources Can Help

- **Enhancing Digital Security:** Tools like antivirus software and encryption can protect your devices and data from unauthorized access and cyber threats.

- **Simplifying Security Management:** Password managers and 2FA apps can streamline the process of maintaining strong, unique passwords and securing your accounts.

- **Protecting Personal Information:** Adjusting privacy settings and using secure browsing tools can help prevent your personal information from being exposed or misused.

- **Staying Educated:** Educational resources keep you informed about emerging threats and best practices, empowering you to take proactive measures to protect yourself.

The Role of Proactive Measures

Proactive measures are crucial in maintaining digital security. Rather than reacting to threats after they occur, using the right tools and resources helps you stay one step ahead of cybercriminals. By implementing these solutions, you create a robust security framework that can adapt to new challenges and evolving threats.

Building a Personal Security Toolkit

Creating a personal security toolkit involves selecting and implementing a combination of tools and resources that suit your needs and lifestyle. This toolkit should be comprehensive yet manageable, ensuring that you can effectively use and maintain each component. The goal is to create a multi-layered defense strategy that covers all aspects of your digital life.

Adapting to New Threats

Cybersecurity is not a one-time effort but an ongoing process. As new threats emerge, it's essential to stay informed and update your tools and practices accordingly. Regularly reviewing and adjusting your security measures ensures that you remain protected against the latest risks.

Collaboration and Community Support

Staying safe online is not an individual effort. Engaging with community groups, participating in forums, and attending educational events can provide additional support and insights. Sharing your experiences and learning from others can enhance your overall security strategy.

By utilizing the tools and resources outlined in this chapter, you can build a robust defense against scams and cyber threats. Remember, the key to effective security is a proactive and informed approach.

Antivirus and Antimalware Software

Antivirus and antimalware software are crucial for protecting your devices from malicious software.

These programs detect, block, and remove viruses, malware, spyware, and other threats, keeping your computer and personal information safe. With the increasing prevalence of cyber threats, having robust antivirus and antimalware protection is essential for maintaining your digital security.

Top Antivirus and Antimalware Software

- **Norton Security**

  - Offers comprehensive protection against viruses, malware, spyware, and other threats.

  - Features include real-time threat protection, firewall, secure VPN, and identity theft protection.

  - **Example:** Norton can help protect your personal information while you browse the internet, shop online, or check emails.

- **McAfee Total Protection**

  - Provides antivirus, identity protection, and

secure browsing features.

- ○ Includes a password manager, file shredder, and encrypted storage.

- ○ **Example:** McAfee's identity protection features can help monitor your personal information and alert you to potential threats.

- **Bitdefender Antivirus Plus**

  - ○ Known for its robust malware detection capabilities.

  - ○ Features include anti-phishing, anti-fraud, and a secure browser for online banking.

  - ○ **Example:** Bitdefender's secure browser ensures that your financial transactions are protected from cyber threats.

- **Malwarebytes**

  - ○ Specializes in malware detection and removal.

  - ○ Can be used alongside other antivirus software for added protection.

- **Example:** Malwarebytes can provide an additional layer of security by detecting and removing malware that other programs might miss.

Tips for Using Antivirus and Antimalware Software

- **Keep Software Updated**

  - Ensure your antivirus and antimalware software are always up to date to protect against the latest threats.

  - **Example:** Enable automatic updates to keep your software current.

- **Run Regular Scans**

  - Schedule regular scans to check your system for malware and other threats.

  - **Example:** Set your software to perform a full scan once a week.

- **Use Real-Time Protection**

○ Enable real-time protection to monitor your system continuously and block threats as they occur.

○ **Example:** Make sure real-time scanning is activated in your software settings.

- **Avoid Multiple Antivirus Programs**

  ○ Using multiple antivirus programs simultaneously can cause conflicts and reduce effectiveness.

  ○ **Example:** Choose one comprehensive antivirus program and supplement it with antimalware software if needed.

How to Choose the Right Software

- **Assess Your Needs**

  ○ Consider what features are most important to you, such as real-time protection, phishing protection, or identity theft protection.

- **Example:** If you do a lot of online banking, choose software with robust anti-phishing features.

- **Read Reviews and Ratings**

  - Research and read reviews from reputable sources to find the best software for your needs.

  - **Example:** Websites like PCMag, CNET, and Consumer Reports offer detailed reviews and ratings.

- **Try Free Trials**

  - Many antivirus programs offer free trials. Take advantage of these to test the software and see if it meets your needs.

  - **Example:** Download a 30-day trial of Norton Security to evaluate its features.

Additional Resources for Antivirus and Antimalware Software

- **AV-Comparatives:** Provides independent tests and reviews of antivirus software.

- **VirusTotal:** Allows you to scan files and URLs for malware using multiple antivirus engines at https://www.virustotal.com.

By using reputable antivirus and antimalware software, you can protect your devices from malicious threats and keep your personal information secure. Regular updates and scans are essential to maintaining this protection.

Password Managers

Creating and remembering strong, unique passwords for all your accounts can be challenging. Password managers solve this problem by securely storing your passwords and generating strong ones for you. This ensures that your accounts are well-protected without the need to remember multiple complex passwords.

Top Password Managers

- **LastPass**

  - Offers both free and premium versions with features like password storage, secure notes, and form filling.

  - **Example:** LastPass can store your login credentials and autofill them when you visit websites, saving you time and effort.

- **1Password**

  - Known for its user-friendly interface and robust security features, including a password generator and secure document storage.

  - **Example:** 1Password's Watchtower feature alerts you to potential security issues, such as compromised websites.

- **Dashlane**

  - Offers a comprehensive security dash-board, dark web monitoring, and secure password storage.

  - **Example:** Dashlane can monitor the dark web for your personal information and alert you if your data is found.

- **Bitwarden**

  - An open-source password manager with features like password storage, secure notes, and two-factor authentication (2FA) integration.

  - **Example:** Bitwarden's open-source nature allows for greater transparency and trust in its security measures.

Benefits of Using Password Managers

- **Strong Password Generation**

  - Password managers can generate complex

passwords that are difficult for hackers to guess.

- ○ **Example:** Instead of using "Password123," a password manager might generate "E8@r&L4o9z!M7h."

- **Secure Storage**

  - ○ Password managers store your passwords in an encrypted vault, protecting them from unauthorized access.

  - ○ **Example:** Your passwords are encrypted with a master password that only you know.

- **Ease of Use**

  - ○ Password managers can autofill your login credentials, making it easy to log into your accounts without manually entering passwords.

  - ○ **Example:** When you visit a website, the password manager fills in your username and password automatically.

- **Cross-Platform Syncing**

○ Most password managers sync across multiple devices, ensuring you have access to your passwords wherever you go.

○ **Example:** You can access your passwords on your computer, smartphone, and tablet seamlessly.

How to Choose the Right Password Manager

- **Assess Your Needs**

  ○ Determine what features are most important to you, such as secure notes, 2FA integration, or dark web monitoring.

  ○ **Example:** If you need to store sensitive documents securely, choose a password manager with document storage capabilities.

- **Read Reviews and Compare Features**

  ○ Research and compare different password managers to find one that meets your needs and preferences.

- **Example:** Websites like PCMag, CNET, and Consumer Reports provide detailed reviews and comparisons of password managers.

- **Try Free Versions or Trials**

  - Many password managers offer free versions or trial periods for their premium features. Use these to test the software and see if it fits your needs.

  - **Example:** Try the free version of LastPass to see if you like its interface and features before upgrading to premium.

Tips for Using Password Managers Effectively

- **Set a Strong Master Password**

  - Your master password is the key to your password vault. Ensure it is strong and unique.

  - **Example:** Use a combination of uppercase and lowercase letters, numbers, and special characters for your master password.

- **Enable Two-Factor Authentication (2FA)**

  - Add an extra layer of security to your password manager by enabling 2FA.

  - **Example:** Use an authentication app like Google Authenticator to generate 2FA codes for your password manager.

- **Regularly Update Your Passwords**

  - Periodically update your passwords to enhance security, especially for sensitive accounts like banking and email.

  - **Example:** Set reminders to change your passwords every few months.

- **Store Backup Codes Securely**

  - If your password manager provides backup codes for account recovery, store them in a secure place.

  - **Example:** Write down backup codes and keep them in a locked safe.

Additional Resources for Password Managers

- **PasswordManager.com:** Provides reviews and comparisons of various password managers at www.**PasswordManager.com**.

- **StaySafeOnline:** Offers tips and resources for creating and managing strong passwords at https://staysafeonline.org/.

By using a reputable password manager, you can ensure your accounts are protected with strong, unique passwords without the hassle of remembering them all. Regularly updating your passwords and enabling 2FA further enhances your security.

***

Privacy Settings

Adjusting privacy settings on your devices and online accounts is essential for protecting your personal information. Proper privacy settings can help prevent unauthorized access, data breaches, and the misuse of your personal data. By understanding and configuring these settings, you can control who sees your information and how it is used.

Key Areas to Adjust Privacy Settings

- **Social Media Accounts**

  - Social media platforms often collect and share a lot of personal information. Adjusting your privacy settings can help limit what is shared publicly and protect your personal data.

- **Web Browsers**

  - Web browsers store a significant amount of information about your online activities. Adjusting browser privacy settings can enhance your online privacy.

- **Mobile Devices**

- Mobile devices store personal information and track your activities through various apps. Adjusting privacy settings on your smartphone or tablet can protect your data.

- **Online Accounts**

  - Adjusting privacy settings on online accounts, such as email, shopping, and banking, can help protect your personal information and enhance security.

Steps to Adjust Privacy Settings

- **Review Privacy Policies**

  - Before using a service or platform, review its privacy policy to understand how your data will be used and protected.

  - **Example:** Read the privacy policy of a new social media app before creating an account.

- **Access Privacy Settings**

- Navigate to the privacy settings section of the platform or device. This is usually found in the settings menu.

- **Example:** On Facebook, go to Settings > Privacy to access and adjust your privacy settings.

- **Adjust Settings According to Your Preferences**

  - Customize the settings to match your privacy preferences. Limit who can see your information and control data sharing.

  - **Example:** On your smartphone, adjust app permissions to restrict access to your contacts and location.

- **Regularly Review and Update Settings**

  - Privacy settings can change with updates. Regularly review and update your settings to ensure they still meet your preferences.

  - **Example:** Periodically check your social media privacy settings to ensure they haven't reverted to default settings after an update.

Benefits of Proper Privacy Settings

- **Enhanced Security**

  - Protects your personal information from unauthorized access and potential data breaches.

  - **Example:** Limiting who can see your social media posts reduces the risk of identity theft.

- **Control Over Personal Data**

  - Gives you control over how your personal data is collected, used, and shared.

  - **Example:** Adjusting ad preferences limits how your data is used for targeted advertising.

- **Reduced Risk of Scams and Phishing**

  - Proper privacy settings can reduce the risk

of falling victim to scams and phishing attacks.

- ○ **Example:** Restricting who can message
  you on social media can reduce unsolicited
  contact from scammers.

Additional Resources for Privacy Settings

- **StaySafeOnline:** Offers tips and guides for
  adjusting privacy settings on various platforms at https://staysafeonline.org/.

- **Electronic Frontier Foundation (EFF):** Provides resources and tools for enhancing your
  online privacy at https://www.eff.org/.

- **Privacy Rights Clearinghouse:** Offers information on protecting your privacy and managing your personal data at https://privacyri
  ghts.org/.

By adjusting your privacy settings on social media,
web browsers, mobile devices, and online accounts,

you can better protect your personal information and control how it is used. Regularly reviewing and updating these settings ensures that your privacy preferences are maintained.

***

Secure Browsing Tools

Browsing the internet safely is crucial for protecting your personal information and avoiding scams, malware, and phishing attempts. Secure browsing tools help enhance your online security by protecting your data, blocking malicious websites, and ensuring that your online activities remain private.

Key Secure Browsing Tools

- **Virtual Private Networks (VPNs)**

  - VPNs encrypt your internet connection, providing privacy and security by hiding your IP address and encrypting your online activities.

- **Example:** Using a VPN can protect your data when connected to public Wi-Fi networks, making it harder for hackers to intercept your information.

- **Browser Extensions**

  - Browser extensions can enhance your browsing security by blocking ads, preventing tracking, and detecting malicious websites.

  - **Example:** Extensions like uBlock Origin, Privacy Badger, and HTTPS Everywhere can improve your online security.

- **Secure Browsers**

  - Some web browsers are specifically designed to offer enhanced security features and privacy protections.

  - **Example:** Browsers like Brave, Tor Browser, and Mozilla Firefox focus on user privacy and security.

- **Anti-Phishing Tools**

  - Anti-phishing tools can help detect and block phishing attempts, protecting you from fraudulent websites that try to steal your personal information.

  - **Example:** Tools like Norton Safe Web and McAfee WebAdvisor provide alerts about suspicious websites and phishing attempts.

Benefits of Using Secure Browsing Tools

- **Enhanced Privacy**

  - Secure browsing tools help protect your privacy by hiding your online activities from prying eyes and preventing tracking.

  - **Example:** A VPN hides your IP address, making it difficult for websites and advertisers to track your browsing habits.

- **Protection Against Malicious Websites**

- These tools can block access to malicious websites, preventing malware infections and phishing attacks.

- **Example:** Browser extensions like uBlock Origin block ads that might contain malware.

- **Secure Data Transmission**

  - VPNs and secure browsers encrypt your data, ensuring that your sensitive information remains safe from interception.

  - **Example:** Using HTTPS Everywhere forces websites to use encrypted connections, protecting your data during transmission.

How to Choose the Right Secure Browsing Tools

- **Assess Your Needs**

  - Determine what features are most important to you, such as encryption, ad blocking, or anti-phishing protection.

- **Example:** If you frequently use public Wi-Fi, a VPN might be a crucial tool for you.

- **Read Reviews and Compare Features**

  - Research and compare different tools to find the ones that best meet your needs and preferences.

  - **Example:** Websites like PCMag, CNET, and TechRadar provide reviews and comparisons of VPNs and browser extensions.

- **Try Free Versions or Trials**

  - Many secure browsing tools offer free versions or trial periods. Use these to test the tools and see if they meet your requirements.

  - **Example:** Try the free version of Proton-VPN to evaluate its features and performance.

Tips for Using Secure Browsing Tools Effectively

- **Keep Software Updated**

  - Ensure your secure browsing tools are always up to date to protect against the latest threats.

  - **Example:** Enable automatic updates for your VPN and browser extensions.

- **Use Multiple Tools for Comprehensive Protection**

  - Combine different tools to cover all aspects of secure browsing, such as a VPN for encryption and a browser extension for ad blocking.

  - **Example:** Use a VPN along with browser extensions like Privacy Badger and HTTPS Everywhere.

- **Be Cautious of Free Tools**

  - While many free tools offer good protection, some may compromise your privacy or have limited features. Choose reputable tools with positive reviews.

  - **Example:** Research free VPNs to ensure

they have a good reputation and don't sell your data.

- **Adjust Settings for Maximum Security**

  - Customize the settings of your secure browsing tools to enhance their effectiveness and tailor them to your needs.

  - **Example:** Configure your VPN to automatically connect when using public Wi-Fi networks.

Additional Resources for Secure Browsing

- **StaySafeOnline:** Offers tips and resources for safe internet browsing at https://staysaf eonline.org/.

- **EFF's Privacy Badger:** A browser extension that blocks trackers and enhances privacy at https://privacybadger.org/.

- **VPN Mentor:** Provides reviews and comparisons of various VPN services at https://www .vpnmentor.com/.

By using secure browsing tools like VPNs, browser extensions, and secure browsers, you can protect your online activities, enhance your privacy, and avoid malicious websites. Regular updates and the right combination of tools will help you maintain a high level of security while browsing the internet.

Encryption Tools

Encryption tools protect your data by converting it into a code that can only be accessed by someone with the decryption key. This ensures that your sensitive information remains confidential and secure, even if it is intercepted by unauthorized parties. Using encryption tools is essential for safeguarding personal information, especially when transmitting data online or storing it on your devices.

Types of Encryption Tools

- **File and Folder Encryption**

  - Tools that encrypt individual files or folders to protect sensitive information on your computer.

  - **Example:** VeraCrypt allows you to create encrypted volumes and encrypt individual files or folders for enhanced security.

- **Full Disk Encryption**

  - Encrypts the entire contents of a hard drive, providing comprehensive protection for all data stored on the device.

  - **Example:** BitLocker (for Windows) and FileVault (for macOS) are built-in tools that offer full disk encryption.

- **Email Encryption**

  - Tools that encrypt the contents of your emails, ensuring that only the intended recipient can read them.

  - **Example:** ProtonMail offers end-to-end

encrypted email services for secure communication.

- **Messaging Encryption**

  - Applications that provide encrypted mes-
    saging to protect your conversations from
    being intercepted.

  - **Example:** Signal and WhatsApp use
    end-to-end encryption to secure your mes-
    sages and calls.

- **Cloud Storage Encryption**

  - Encrypts data before it is uploaded to
    cloud storage services, ensuring that your
    information remains secure even if the
    cloud provider is compromised.

  - **Example:** Tresorit offers secure,
    end-to-end encrypted cloud storage.

Benefits of Using Encryption Tools

- **Confidentiality**

- Encryption ensures that your data can only be accessed by authorized individuals with the decryption key.

- **Example:** Encrypting sensitive documents ensures that only you and those you trust can read them.

- **Security**

  - Protects your data from unauthorized access, even if it is intercepted or stolen.

  - **Example:** Encrypting your hard drive protects your data if your computer is lost or stolen.

- **Compliance**

  - Helps you comply with data protection regulations that require the encryption of sensitive information.

  - **Example:** Businesses must encrypt customer data to comply with regulations like GDPR or HIPAA.

How to Choose the Right Encryption Tools

- **Determine Your Needs**

  - Identify what type of data you need to encrypt and choose tools that best meet those needs.

  - **Example:** If you need to encrypt email communications, choose an email encryption service like ProtonMail.

- **Evaluate Ease of Use**

  - Choose encryption tools that are user-friendly and easy to implement.

  - **Example:** BitLocker and FileVault are integrated into Windows and macOS, making them easy to set up and use.

- **Check Compatibility**

  - Ensure that the encryption tools are compatible with your operating system and devices.

  - **Example:** VeraCrypt is compatible with

Windows, macOS, and Linux, making it a versatile option for file encryption.

- **Consider Additional Features**

  - Look for tools that offer additional features, such as secure file sharing or multi-device support.

  - **Example:** Tresorit not only encrypts your files but also offers secure file sharing and collaboration features.

Tips for Using Encryption Tools Effectively

- **Keep Your Encryption Keys Secure**

  - Store your encryption keys or passwords in a secure location. Losing them means you cannot access your encrypted data.

  - **Example:** Use a password manager to store and manage your encryption keys securely.

- **Regularly Update Your Encryption Soft-**

ware

- ○ Ensure that your encryption software is up to date to protect against vulnerabilities and new threats.

- ○ **Example:** Enable automatic updates for your encryption tools to keep them current.

- **Back Up Your Encrypted Data**

  - ○ Regularly back up your encrypted data to prevent data loss in case of hardware failure or other issues.

  - ○ **Example:** Store backups of encrypted files on an external drive or a secure cloud service.

- **Educate Yourself on Encryption Best Practices**

  - ○ Stay informed about the latest encryption standards and best practices to ensure your data remains secure.

  - ○ **Example:** Follow reputable cybersecurity blogs and resources to keep up with encryption trends and tips.

Additional Resources for Encryption Tools

- **Electronic Frontier Foundation (EFF):** Provides guides and resources on encryption and digital privacy at https://www.eff.org/.

- **StaySafeOnline:** Offers tips and information on using encryption to protect your data at https://staysafeonline.org/.

- **VeraCrypt Documentation:** Detailed guides on using VeraCrypt for file and folder encryption at https://www.veracrypt.fr/en/Documentation.html.

By using encryption tools, you can protect your sensitive information from unauthorized access and ensure that your data remains confidential. Regularly updating your encryption software and following best practices will help maintain the security of your encrypted data.

***

Two-Factor Authentication (2FA) Apps

Two-Factor Authentication (2FA) provides an additional layer of security for your online accounts by requiring a second form of verification in addition to your password. This significantly reduces the risk of unauthorized access, even if your password is compromised. 2FA apps generate time-based codes or send push notifications to your mobile device, ensuring that only you can access your accounts.

Top Two-Factor Authentication Apps

- **Google Authenticator**
  - Generates time-based one-time passwords (TOTP) for your accounts.
  - **Example:** Use Google Authenticator to generate 2FA codes for your email, social

media, and banking accounts.

- **Authy**

  - Offers encrypted backups and multi-device synchronization for your 2FA codes.

  - **Example:** Authy allows you to access your 2FA codes on multiple devices, providing a convenient and secure solution.

- **Microsoft Authenticator**

  - Supports TOTP and push notifications for Microsoft accounts and other services.

  - **Example:** Use Microsoft Authenticator for your Microsoft accounts and other online services that support 2FA.

- **Duo Mobile**

  - Provides push notifications, TOTP codes, and integration with various online services.

  - **Example:** Duo Mobile is commonly used by organizations for securing employee accounts and can be used for personal accounts as well.

- **LastPass Authenticator**

  - Integrates with LastPass Password Manager and offers TOTP codes and push notifications.

  - **Example:** LastPass Authenticator is a convenient option if you already use LastPass for password management.

Benefits of Using 2FA Apps

- **Enhanced Security**

  - Adds a second layer of protection to your accounts, making it harder for unauthorized users to gain access.

  - **Example:** Even if someone steals your password, they would still need the 2FA code to access your account.

- **Easy to Use**

- 2FA apps are user-friendly and provide quick access to verification codes.

- **Example:** Simply open the app to view the current code and enter it when prompted during login.

- **Multi-Device Support**

  - Many 2FA apps offer support for multiple devices, ensuring you can access your codes from your smartphone, tablet, or computer.

  - **Example:** Authy allows you to sync your 2FA codes across multiple devices securely.

- **Backup and Recovery**

  - Some 2FA apps offer encrypted backups, making it easy to recover your codes if you lose your device.

  - **Example:** Authy provides encrypted backups and a recovery process to restore your 2FA codes on a new device.

How to Choose the Right 2FA App

- **Evaluate Compatibility**

  - Ensure the 2FA app is compatible with the services and accounts you use.

  - **Example:** Google Authenticator and Authy are compatible with a wide range of services, including Google, Facebook, and Dropbox.

- **Consider Multi-Device Support**

  - Choose an app that offers multi-device support if you need access to your codes on more than one device.

  - **Example:** Authy and Duo Mobile offer multi-device synchronization for added convenience.

- **Check for Backup and Recovery Options**

  - Select an app that provides backup and recovery options to prevent losing access to your accounts.

- **Example:** Authy and LastPass Authenticator offer encrypted backups and recovery features.

- **Assess User Interface and Ease of Use**

  - Choose an app with a user-friendly interface that makes it easy to generate and enter 2FA codes.

  - **Example:** Microsoft Authenticator and Google Authenticator are known for their simple and intuitive interfaces.

Tips for Using 2FA Apps Effectively

- **Enable 2FA on All Important Accounts**

  - Use 2FA for email, banking, social media, and any other accounts containing sensitive information.

  - **Example:** Enable 2FA for your Gmail, Facebook, and online banking accounts.

- **Keep Your 2FA App Secure**

- Protect your 2FA app with a strong password or biometric lock (fingerprint or facial recognition) if supported.

- **Example:** Use a fingerprint lock on your smartphone to secure your 2FA app.

- **Store Backup Codes Securely**

  - Many services provide backup codes during 2FA setup. Store these codes in a secure location for account recovery.

  - **Example:** Write down backup codes and keep them in a locked safe.

- **Regularly Review and Update 2FA Settings**

  - Periodically review your 2FA settings and update them if necessary to ensure optimal security.

  - **Example:** Check your 2FA settings on your online accounts and update any outdated information.

Additional Resources for Two-Factor Authentication

- **TwoFactorAuth.org:** A comprehensive list of websites and services that support 2FA at https://brainstation.io/cybersecurity/two-factor-auth.

- **StaySafeOnline:** Offers tips and resources for implementing 2FA on your accounts at https://staysafeonline.org/.

- **Google Security Blog:** Provides updates and best practices for using Google Authenticator and other security tools at https://security.googleblog.com/.

By using 2FA apps, you can significantly enhance the security of your online accounts and protect your personal information from unauthorized access. Regularly updating your 2FA settings and using backup codes will ensure you maintain access to your accounts even in the event of device loss or failure.

Educational Resources

Staying educated about the latest scams, cybersecurity threats, and best practices is crucial for protecting yourself and your personal information. Educational resources can help you stay informed, recognize potential threats, and take proactive steps to enhance your security. By continuously learning about cybersecurity, you can adapt to new challenges and better safeguard your digital life.

Top Educational Resources for Cybersecurity and Scam Awareness

- **Federal Trade Commission (FTC)**

  - The FTC provides comprehensive information on various types of scams, identity theft, and consumer protection. Their website offers resources, tips, and guides to help you stay informed.

- **Example:** Visit the FTC's website for up-dates on recent scams and practical advice on avoiding fraud at https://consumer.ftc .gov/scams.

- **AARP Fraud Watch Network**

  - AARP's Fraud Watch Network offers re-sources specifically designed for seniors. They provide information on common scams targeting older adults and tips for protecting yourself.

  - **Example:** Sign up for AARP's Fraud Watch Network alerts to receive updates on the latest scams and fraud prevention tips at https://www.aarp.org/money/scams-fr aud/about-fraud-watch-network/.

- **StaySafeOnline**

  - Operated by the National Cyber Securi-ty Alliance, StaySafeOnline provides re-sources and tips for safe internet brows-ing, protecting personal information, and preventing cybercrime.

- **Example:** Explore StaySafeOnline's website for educational materials on online safety and cybersecurity best practices at https://staysafeonline.org/.

- **Better Business Bureau (BBB)**

  - The BBB offers information on scams, consumer alerts, and tips for avoiding fraud. They also provide a Scam Tracker tool to report and track scams in your area.

  - **Example:** Use the BBB Scam Tracker to stay informed about local scams and report suspicious activities at https://www.bbb.org/scamtracker.

- **Cybersecurity and Infrastructure Security Agency (CISA)**

  - CISA provides resources and guidance on cybersecurity threats, best practices, and emergency response. Their website includes alerts, newsletters, and educational materials.

  - **Example:** Visit CISA's website for cybersecurity alerts and comprehensive guides on

protecting your digital assets at https://w
ww.cisa.gov/.

- **Consumer Reports**

  - Consumer Reports offers articles, reviews,
    and guides on various consumer products,
    including cybersecurity tools. They provide
    insights into the latest scams and how to
    protect yourself.

  - **Example:** Read Consumer Reports' re-
    views on antivirus software and password
    managers to make informed decisions at
    https://www.consumerreports.org/.

Benefits of Using Educational Resources

- **Awareness of Latest Threats**

  - Staying updated on the latest scams and
    cybersecurity threats helps you recognize
    and avoid potential dangers.

  - **Example:** Regularly reading FTC alerts
    keeps you informed about new phishing

tactics and how to avoid them.

- **Practical Tips and Advice**

  - Educational resources provide practical tips and step-by-step guides for protecting your personal information and enhancing your security.

  - **Example:** StaySafeOnline offers practical advice on creating strong passwords and using two-factor authentication.

- **Empowerment and Confidence**

  - Knowledge empowers you to take control of your digital security and confidently navigate the online world.

  - **Example:** Understanding common scam tactics makes you less likely to fall victim to fraud.

- **Community Support**

  - Many educational resources offer community forums and support networks where you can share experiences and learn from others.

- **Example:** Participating in the AARP Fraud Watch Network community can provide support and advice from fellow seniors.

How to Utilize Educational Resources Effectively

- **Subscribe to Newsletters and Alerts**

  - Sign up for newsletters and alerts from reputable sources to receive regular updates on scams and cybersecurity threats.

  - **Example:** Subscribe to the FTC's consumer alerts and AARP's Fraud Watch Network newsletters.

- **Attend Webinars and Workshops**

  - Participate in webinars and workshops offered by organizations like StaySafeOnline and CISA to learn about cybersecurity best practices and emerging threats.

  - **Example:** Attend a StaySafeOnline webinar on protecting your personal information during online shopping.

- **Engage with Online Communities**

  - Join online forums and communities focused on cybersecurity and scam prevention to share experiences and learn from others.

  - **Example:** Participate in discussions on the AARP Fraud Watch Network community forum.

- **Read Articles and Guides**

  - Regularly read articles, guides, and reviews from reputable sources to stay informed about the latest security tools and practices.

  - **Example:** Explore Consumer Reports' articles on choosing the best antivirus software for your needs.

- **Share Knowledge with Others**

  - Share what you've learned with friends and family to help them stay informed and protect themselves from scams and cyber threats.

○ **Example:** Discuss recent scam alerts with your loved ones and share tips on how to avoid fraud.

Additional Resources for Staying Educated

- **Krebs on Security:** A blog by cybersecurity expert Brian Krebs, offering in-depth analysis and updates on the latest cyber threats at https://krebsonsecurity.com/.

- **SANS Internet Storm Center:** Provides daily reports on cybersecurity incidents and threats, along with educational resources at https://isc.sans.edu/.

- **Norton Security Center:** Offers articles, tips, and guides on various cybersecurity topics, including phishing, malware, and identity theft at https://us.norton.com/blog.

By utilizing educational resources and staying informed, you can enhance your cybersecurity knowledge and protect yourself from scams and cyber threats. Regular engagement with these resources will keep you updated on the latest developments and best practices in digital security.

Five

Responding to a Threat

Even with the best precautions, you might still encounter a scam or a security threat. Knowing how to respond effectively can minimize damage and help you recover more quickly. This chapter will guide you through the steps to take if you suspect a scam, experience identity theft, or face other security threats. By being prepared and understanding the appropriate actions, you can protect yourself and limit the impact of these incidents.

Why Responding to Threats is Crucial

Despite your best efforts to stay safe, cyber threats and scams are constantly evolving. Scammers use sophisticated tactics to trick even the most cautious individuals. When you encounter such threats, timely and effective response is crucial to mitigate potential damage. Understanding how to recognize and respond to these threats empowers you to take control of the situation, protect your assets, and prevent further harm.

Overview of This Chapter

This chapter covers the essential steps you need to take when confronted with different types of security threats. We will explore:

- **Recognizing and Responding to Scams:**
  - Identifying common signs of scams and taking immediate action to protect yourself.

- **Reporting Mechanisms:**

  - Understanding how and where to report scams to the appropriate authorities.

- **Recovering from Identity Theft:**

  - Steps to take if your personal information has been compromised, including contacting financial institutions, placing fraud alerts, and using identity theft recovery resources.

- **Handling Financial Fraud:**

  - Addressing unauthorized transactions and securing your financial accounts to prevent further loss.

- **Utilizing Support and Resources:**

  - Accessing additional resources and support systems to aid in recovery and prevention.

The Emotional and Practical Aspects

Facing a scam or security threat can be overwhelming and stressful. It's important to address both the emotional and practical aspects of the situation. Emotional support from friends, family, or professional counselors can help you cope with the stress and anxiety. Practically, having a clear plan of action and knowing the right steps to take can significantly reduce the impact of the threat and expedite your recovery.

Taking Preventive Measures

While this chapter focuses on responding to threats, it's essential to remember that preventive measures are your first line of defense. Regularly updating your knowledge about the latest scams, maintaining robust security practices, and using protective tools can help minimize the likelihood of encountering threats. However, should you find yourself facing a scam or security breach, being informed and prepared will enable you to respond effectively.

By understanding the steps outlined in this chapter, you will be better equipped to handle any security threats that come your way, ensuring that you can quickly and effectively protect yourself and your personal information.

***

What to Do If You Suspect a Scam

Recognizing the Signs

If you suspect you are being targeted by a scam, it's important to recognize the warning signs and take immediate action. Common signs include unsolicited requests for personal information, pressure to act quickly, and offers that seem too good to be true.

Steps to Take

- **Stop Communication Immediately**

  - If you suspect a scam, stop all communication with the potential scammer. Do not respond to emails, phone calls, or messages.

  - **Example:** If you receive a suspicious email asking for personal information, do not reply or click on any links.

- **Do Not Share Personal Information**

  - Avoid providing any personal or financial information to the suspected scammer.

  - **Example:** If someone asks for your Social Security number or bank account details, do not provide them.

- **Verify the Source**

  - Contact the organization or person directly using verified contact information to confirm the legitimacy of the request.

  - **Example:** If you receive a call from someone claiming to be from your bank, call the bank's customer service number listed on their official website to verify.

- **Report the Scam**

  - Report the suspected scam to the appropriate authorities, such as the Federal Trade Commission (FTC), Better Business Bureau (BBB), or your local law enforcement.

  - **Example:** File a complaint with the FTC at www.ftc.gov/complaint.

- **Warn Others**

  - Share your experience with friends and family to warn them about the potential scam and help them avoid falling victim.

  - **Example:** Post about the scam on social media or discuss it with loved ones to raise awareness.

- **Document Everything**

  - Keep records of all communications and transactions related to the suspected scam. This information can be helpful when reporting the scam and seeking assistance.

- **Example:** Save emails, take screenshots of text messages, and note down any relevant details from phone calls.

Real-Life Example of Responding to a Suspected Scam

Consider the case of Jane, who received an email from someone claiming to be from her bank, asking her to verify her account information to avoid suspension. Sensing something was off, Jane did not click on the link in the email. Instead, she called her bank using the number on the back of her debit card. The bank confirmed that no such email had been sent and advised her to report the phishing attempt to the FTC. Jane also shared her experience with her friends and family to alert them to the scam.

Why Immediate Action is Important

Acting quickly when you suspect a scam can prevent further damage and protect your personal information. Scammers rely on creating a sense of urgency to prompt immediate responses, so taking a step back to verify the situation can make a significant difference.

By following these steps, you can effectively respond to suspected scams, protect your personal information, and help others avoid similar threats.

Reporting Mechanisms

Reporting scams and security threats helps authorities track and combat fraud, prevents others from falling victim, and may assist in recovering lost assets. It also contributes to a broader understanding of current scam trends and helps create more effective prevention strategies.

How to Report Different Types of Scams

- **Online Scams**

  - Report online scams, such as phishing emails and fraudulent websites, to the FTC and the Internet Crime Complaint Center (IC3).

  - **Example:** If you receive a phishing email, forward it to the FTC at spam@uce.gov and report it to IC3 at www.ic3.gov.

- **Phone Scams**

  - Report phone scams, including IRS imper-sonation and tech support scams, to the FTC and your phone service provider.

  - **Example:** If you receive a scam call, report it to the FTC and your phone provider's fraud department.

- **Identity Theft**

  - Report identity theft to the FTC and your local police department. Use the FTC's Ide ntityTheft.gov website for a recovery plan.

- **Example:** If you notice unauthorized charges on your credit card, report the fraud to the FTC and file a police report.

- **Mail Scams**

  - Report mail scams, such as lottery or sweepstakes scams, to the United States Postal Inspection Service (USPIS).

  - **Example:** If you receive a fraudulent letter claiming you've won a prize, report it to USPIS at www.uspis.gov.

Steps to Take When Reporting

- **Gather Information**

  - Collect all relevant information, including emails, messages, phone numbers, and any other communication from the scammer.

  - **Example:** Save copies of emails and take

screenshots of text messages related to the scam.

- **File a Report**

  ○ Submit a detailed report to the appropriate authority, providing as much information as possible.

  ○ **Example:** Complete the FTC's online complaint form with all relevant details about the scam.

- **Follow Up**

  ○ Keep track of your report and follow up with the authority if necessary to provide additional information or updates.

  ○ **Example:** If you receive further communication from the scammer, update your report with the new information.

Reporting Resources

- **Federal Trade Commission (FTC)**

- **Website:** www.ftc.gov/complaint

- **Phone:** 1-877-FTC-HELP (1-877-382-4357)

- **Internet Crime Complaint Center (IC3)**

  - **Website:** www.ic3.gov

- **United States Postal Inspection Service (USPIS)**

  - **Website:** www.uspis.gov

  - **Phone:** 1-877-876-2455

- **United States Treasury Inspector General for Tax Administration**

  - **Website:** https://www.tigta.gov/

- **Better Business Bureau (BBB)**

  - **Website:** www.bbb.org/scamtracker

  - **Phone:** Contact your local BBB office

- **Local Law Enforcement**

  - **Contact Information:** Visit your local police department's website or call their non-emergency number

Real-Life Example of Reporting a Scam

Consider the case of John, who received a phone call from someone claiming to be from the IRS, demanding immediate payment for back taxes. Recognizing this as a scam, John ended the call and reported it to the FTC and the Treasury Inspector General for Tax Administration (TIGTA) at https://www.tigta.gov/. He also informed his phone service provider to block the scammer's number. By reporting the scam, John helped authorities track the fraudulent activity and potentially prevent others from falling victim.

The Impact of Reporting

Reporting scams not only helps authorities take action against fraudsters but also raises awareness within the community. The data collected from reports can be used to develop educational resources and preventive measures, contributing to a safer environment for everyone. By taking the time to report scams, you play a crucial role in the fight against fraud and help protect others from becoming victims.

***

Recovering from Identity Theft

Steps to Take Immediately

Identity theft can be overwhelming, but taking immediate action can help minimize damage and start the recovery process. Here's what to do if you suspect your personal information has been compromised:

- **Contact Financial Institutions**
  - Notify your bank, credit card companies, and other financial institutions of the identity theft. Request that they close or freeze

affected accounts.

- **Example:** Call your bank's fraud department to report unauthorized transactions and request a freeze on your account.

- **Place a Fraud Alert on Your Credit Reports**

  - Contact the three major credit bureaus (Equifax, Experian, TransUnion) to place a fraud alert on your credit report. This makes it harder for identity thieves to open new accounts in your name.

  - **Example:** Call Equifax to place a fraud alert, and they will notify the other two bureaus.

- **File a Report with the FTC**

  - Use the FTC's IdentityTheft.gov website to report the identity theft and create a recovery plan.

  - **Example:** Complete the FTC's identity theft report and follow their step-by-step recovery guide.

- **File a Police Report**

- Report the identity theft to your local police department. Provide them with a copy of your FTC report and any other relevant information.

- **Example:** Visit your local police station with documentation to file a report.

- **Close Fraudulent Accounts**

  - Contact the companies where the fraudulent accounts were opened. Explain that the account was opened fraudulently and ask them to close or freeze the accounts.

  - **Example:** If an identity thief opened a credit card account in your name, contact the credit card company to close the account and dispute any charges.

Steps to Take for Ongoing Protection

- **Monitor Your Credit Reports**

  - Regularly check your credit reports for any unauthorized activity or new accounts you did not open.

- ○ **Example:** Request a free credit report from each of the three credit bureaus annually through AnnualCreditReport.com.

- **Use Identity Theft Protection Services**

  - ○ Consider enrolling in an identity theft protection service that offers credit monitoring, alerts, and recovery assistance.

  - ○ **Example:** Services like LifeLock and IdentityForce provide comprehensive identity theft protection.

- **Update Security Practices**

  - ○ Strengthen your security practices, such as using strong passwords, enabling two-factor authentication, and being cautious with your personal information.

  - ○ **Example:** Change passwords for all your online accounts and enable two-factor authentication where possible.

- **Secure Your Personal Information**

- Take steps to protect your personal information, such as shredding sensitive documents, using secure mailboxes, and being cautious about sharing information online.

- **Example:** Use a cross-cut shredder to destroy documents containing personal information before disposing of them.

Additional Resources for Recovering from Identity Theft

- **IdentityTheft.gov:** The FTC's online resource for reporting identity theft and creating a recovery plan at https://www.identitytheft.gov/.

- **Equifax, Experian, and TransUnion:** Contact these credit bureaus to place fraud alerts and monitor your credit reports.

  - **Equifax:** www.equifax.com or 1-800-525-6285

  - **Experian:** www.experian.com or

1-888-397-3742

- ○ **TransUnion:** www.transunion.com or 1-800-680-7289

- **Local Police Department:** File a police report to document the identity theft and assist with the recovery process.

- **Consumer Financial Protection Bureau (CFPB):** Provides additional resources and guidance on recovering from identity theft at https://www.consumerfinance.gov/.

Real-Life Example of Recovering from Identity Theft

Consider the case of Emily, who discovered unauthorized charges on her credit card statement. She immediately contacted her bank to report the fraud and requested a freeze on her account. Emily then placed a fraud alert on her credit reports by contacting Equifax, which notified the other two bureaus. She filed a report with the FTC through IdentityThef t.gov and created a recovery plan. Finally, Emily filed a police report to document the incident. By taking these steps, Emily was able to address the immediate threat and implement measures to protect her identity moving forward.

By following these steps, you can effectively respond to identity theft, minimize damage, and take control of the recovery process. Regular monitoring and updating your security practices will help prevent future incidents.

***

Handling Financial Fraud

Steps to Take Immediately

If you discover unauthorized transactions or suspect financial fraud, taking immediate action is crucial to limit damage and secure your accounts. Here's what to do:

- **Contact Your Financial Institutions**

- Notify your bank or credit card company immediately about any unauthorized transactions. Request that they freeze or close the affected accounts.

- **Example:** Call your bank's fraud department to report suspicious activity and dispute unauthorized charges.

- **Review Account Statements**

  - Carefully review your recent account statements for any additional unauthorized transactions.

  - **Example:** Look for small test charges that scammers might use to check if an account is active.

- **Change Account Passwords**

  - Change the passwords for any accounts that have been compromised. Use strong, unique passwords and consider using a password manager.

  - **Example:** Update your online banking password and enable two-factor authentication for added security.

- **Monitor Accounts Closely**

  - Keep a close eye on your accounts for further unauthorized activity. Set up account alerts to receive notifications of any unusual transactions.

  - **Example:** Enable text or email alerts for transactions over a certain amount.

Steps to Take for Ongoing Protection

- **Place a Fraud Alert**

  - Contact the three major credit bureaus to place a fraud alert on your credit report. This will notify creditors to take extra steps to verify your identity before opening new accounts.

  - **Example:** Contact Experian to place a fraud alert, and they will notify the other two bureaus.

- **Consider a Credit Freeze**

  - A credit freeze restricts access to your credit report, making it difficult for identity thieves to open new accounts in your name. You can temporarily lift the freeze when you need to apply for credit.

  - **Example:** Place a credit freeze through Equifax, Experian, and TransUnion's websites.

- **File a Police Report**

  - Report the financial fraud to your local police department. Provide them with all relevant information, including bank statements and any communication with the fraudster.

  - **Example:** Visit your local police station with documentation to file a report.

- **Report the Fraud to the FTC**

  - File a complaint with the FTC through I dentityTheft.gov. This will help authorities track fraud patterns and assist in your recovery.

- ◦ **Example:** Use IdentityTheft.gov to create a personalized recovery plan and follow the step-by-step guidance.

Protecting Yourself from Future Financial Fraud

- **Use Secure Payment Methods**

  - ◦ Use credit cards instead of debit cards for online purchases, as they offer better fraud protection.

  - ◦ **Example:** Credit cards typically have zero liability policies for unauthorized charges, unlike debit cards.

- **Enable Two-Factor Authentication**

  - ◦ Enable two-factor authentication (2FA) on your financial accounts to add an extra layer of security.

  - ◦ **Example:** Set up 2FA on your online banking account to require a verification code in addition to your password.

- **Be Cautious with Personal Information**

  - Avoid sharing personal information over the phone, through email, or on social media.

  - **Example:** Never provide your Social Security number or bank account details to unsolicited callers.

- **Shred Sensitive Documents**

  - Shred bank statements, credit card offers, and other documents containing personal information before disposing of them.

  - **Example:** Use a cross-cut shredder to destroy old bank statements and tax documents.

Real-Life Example of Handling Financial Fraud

Consider the case of Mark, who noticed several unauthorized transactions on his credit card statement. Mark immediately contacted his credit card company to report the fraud and requested a freeze on his account. He then reviewed his other accounts for any additional suspicious activity and changed his passwords. Mark also placed a fraud alert on his credit report and filed a complaint with the FTC. By taking these steps, Mark was able to quickly address the financial fraud and prevent further damage.

Additional Resources for Handling Financial Fraud

- **Federal Trade Commission (FTC):** Provides resources and guidance on dealing with financial fraud and identity theft.

  - **Website:** www.identitytheft.gov

  - **Phone:** 1-877-FTC-HELP (1-877-382-4357)

- **Consumer Financial Protection Bureau (CFPB):** Offers information on protecting yourself from financial fraud and resolving disputes.

  - **Website:** www.consumerfinance.gov

- **Phone:** 1-855-411-CFPB (1-855-411-2372)

- **Local Police Department:** File a police report to document the financial fraud and assist with the recovery process.

By following these steps, you can effectively handle financial fraud, secure your accounts, and take measures to prevent future incidents. Regular monitoring and updating your security practices will help you stay protected.

Utilizing Support and Resources

Dealing with scams, identity theft, and financial fraud can be overwhelming and stressful. Utilizing available support and resources can provide guidance, assistance, and peace of mind during the recovery process. Knowing where to find help and understanding the resources at your disposal are crucial steps in effectively responding to and recovering from threats.

Key Support Resources

- **Federal Trade Commission (FTC)**

  - The FTC provides comprehensive resources and tools for reporting scams, recovering from identity theft, and protecting yourself from fraud.

  - **Example:** Use the FTC's IdentityTheft.gov to report identity theft and create a personalized recovery plan.

  - **Website:** www.ftc.gov

- **IdentityTheft.gov**

  - A one-stop resource for victims of identity theft, offering step-by-step guidance on how to report and recover from identity theft.

  - **Example:** Follow the recovery plan provided by IdentityTheft.gov to address all aspects of identity theft.

- **Website:** www.identitytheft.gov

- **Better Business Bureau (BBB)**

  - The BBB offers resources for reporting scams and fraudulent activities, as well as tools to check the legitimacy of businesses.

  - **Example:** Use the BBB Scam Tracker to report a scam and see if others have reported similar experiences.

  - **Website:** www.bbb.org

- **Consumer Financial Protection Bureau (CFPB)**

  - The CFPB provides information and resources to help consumers protect themselves from financial fraud and resolve disputes with financial institutions.

  - **Example:** Visit the CFPB's website for guidance on dealing with unauthorized charges and disputing fraudulent transactions.

- **Website:** www.consumerfinance.gov

- **AARP Fraud Watch Network**

  - AARP's Fraud Watch Network offers resources, alerts, and support specifically designed for seniors to protect themselves from scams and fraud.

  - **Example:** Sign up for AARP's Fraud Watch Network alerts to stay informed about the latest scams targeting seniors.

  - **Website:** www.aarp.org/money/scams-fraud/

- **Local Law Enforcement**

  - Your local police department can provide assistance and support if you are a victim of fraud or identity theft.

  - **Example:** File a police report to document the fraud and receive assistance in recovering your stolen identity.

Emotional Support Resources

- **Friends and Family**

  - Share your experience with trusted friends and family members who can provide emotional support and practical advice.

  - **Example:** Talk to a family member about your experience and ask for their help in dealing with the situation.

- **Support Groups**

  - Join support groups for victims of scams and identity theft. These groups offer a sense of community and understanding from others who have experienced similar situations.

  - **Example:** Look for local or online support groups where you can share your story and receive support.

- **Professional Counseling**

  - Consider seeking professional counseling to help manage the stress and emotional impact of dealing with fraud and identity theft.

- **Example:** A counselor can provide strategies for coping with anxiety and stress related to the incident.

Additional Resources for Ongoing Education and Prevention

- **StaySafeOnline**

  - Offers tips and resources for safe internet browsing, protecting personal information, and preventing cybercrime.

  - **Example:** Explore StaySafeOnline's educational materials on creating strong passwords and avoiding phishing scams.

  - **Website:** www.staysafeonline.org

- **Electronic Frontier Foundation (EFF)**

  - Provides resources and tools for enhancing your online privacy and security.

- **Example:** Use EFF's Privacy Badger browser extension to block trackers and enhance your online privacy.

- **Website:** www.eff.org

• **Consumer Reports**

- Offers articles, reviews, and guides on various consumer products, including cybersecurity tools and services.

- **Example:** Read Consumer Reports' reviews on identity theft protection services to choose the best option for your needs.

- **Website:** www.consumerreports.org

Creating a Personal Security Plan

• **Assess Your Risks**

- Evaluate your personal and financial risks to identify areas where you need to enhance your security.

- ○ **Example:** Identify which of your online accounts are most vulnerable and prioritize securing them with strong passwords and two-factor authentication.

- **Develop a Response Plan**

  - ○ Create a step-by-step plan for responding to different types of security threats, including scams, identity theft, and financial fraud.

  - ○ **Example:** Outline the steps you will take if you discover unauthorized transactions on your bank account.

- **Regularly Update Your Knowledge**

  - ○ Stay informed about the latest scams, cybersecurity threats, and best practices by regularly reading articles, attending webinars, and participating in community discussions.

  - ○ **Example:** Subscribe to newsletters from reputable sources like the FTC and AARP Fraud Watch Network.

- **Share Your Plan with Trusted Contacts**

  - Share your personal security plan with trusted friends or family members who can assist you in case of an emergency.

  - **Example:** Provide a family member with copies of important documents and instructions on how to help you if you become a victim of identity theft.

By utilizing the support and resources available to you, you can effectively respond to scams, identity theft, and financial fraud. Remember, you are not alone, and there are numerous organizations and communities ready to assist you in your recovery and prevention efforts.

Six

Practical Scenarios

Understanding how to apply the knowledge and tools covered in previous chapters is crucial for effectively protecting yourself from scams and security threats. Practical scenarios provide a detailed walkthrough of real-life situations, helping you recognize potential dangers and respond appropriately. By examining these scenarios, you can see how to put theory into practice and gain confidence in your ability to handle similar situations.

Why Practical Scenarios Matter

Practical scenarios bridge the gap between theoretical knowledge and real-world application. They allow you to see how the principles and techniques you've learned are used in everyday situations. This hands-on approach helps reinforce your understanding and prepares you to act swiftly and effectively when faced with a threat.

Benefits of Learning Through Scenarios

- **Enhanced Understanding:**

  - Seeing concepts applied in real-life situations helps solidify your understanding and makes it easier to remember and use these techniques.

- **Improved Confidence:**

  - Practicing responses to common threats builds your confidence, making you more likely to take appropriate action when needed.

- **Preparation for the Unexpected:**

  - By exploring various scenarios, you become better prepared to handle different types of scams and security threats that may come your way.

- **Reinforcement of Best Practices:**

  - Practical scenarios reinforce the importance of best practices, such as verifying information, protecting personal data, and reporting suspicious activity.

Scope of This Chapter

In this chapter, we will cover a range of practical scenarios, each representing a common scam or security threat. For each scenario, we will provide a step-by-step guide on how to recognize the threat, take appropriate action, and protect yourself from harm. These scenarios include:

- **Recognizing a Phishing Email**

- **Handling a Suspicious Phone Call**

- **Identifying a Fake Charity**

- **Dealing with a Tech Support Scam**

- **Recognizing and Avoiding Investment Scams**

- **Responding to a Romance Scam**

- **Avoiding Lottery and Sweepstakes Scams**

- **Handling a Fake Job Offer**

- **Identifying a Utility Scam**

- **Dealing with a Social Media Scam**

- **Responding to a Grandparent Scam**

- **Handling a Health Insurance Scam**

- **Avoiding Home Repair Scams**

- **Spotting an Investment Seminar Scam**

How to Use This Chapter

Refer to the practical scenarios to see how the concepts and tools discussed in previous chapters are applied in real-life situations. Use these scenarios as a guide to help you recognize and respond to threats effectively. Whether you are dealing with a suspicious email, a fraudulent phone call, or any other type of scam, the steps outlined in these scenarios will provide you with the guidance you need to protect yourself.

Building Confidence Through Practice

By familiarizing yourself with practical scenarios, you build the confidence to handle potential threats effectively. Knowing what to look for and how to respond empowers you to take control of your security and protect yourself from scams and fraud.

***

Scenario 1: Recognizing a Phishing Email

Situation:

John receives an email from what appears to be his bank, stating that there has been suspicious activity on his account. The email asks him to click a link and enter his account information to verify his identity.

Steps to Take:

1. **Examine the Sender's Email Address:**

   ○ John checks the sender's email address and notices that it doesn't match the bank's official domain. This is a red flag.

2. **Avoid Clicking on Links:**

   ○ Instead of clicking the link in the email, John opens a new browser window and types in the bank's official website URL directly.

3. **Contact the Bank Directly:**

   ○ John calls the bank's customer service number, found on their official website, to verify if there has been any suspicious activity on his account.

4. **Report the Email:**

  - After confirming with his bank that the email is a phishing attempt, John reports the email to the bank's fraud department and forwards it to the FTC at spam@uce.gov.

5. **Delete the Email:**

  - John deletes the phishing email to prevent any accidental clicks in the future.

✱✱✱

Scenario 2: Handling a Suspicious Phone Call

Situation:
Mary receives a phone call from someone claiming to be from the IRS, stating that she owes back taxes and must pay immediately to avoid arrest. The caller demands payment via gift cards.

Steps to Take:

1. **Stay Calm and Do Not Provide Information:**

   - Mary remains calm and does not provide any personal or financial information to the caller.

2. **Verify the Caller's Identity:**

   - She tells the caller she will call back and hangs up. Mary then looks up the IRS's official phone number on their website.

3. **Contact the IRS Directly:**

   - Mary calls the official IRS number to verify the claim. The IRS confirms that they did not contact her and that the call was a scam.

4. **Report the Call:**

   - Mary reports the scam call to the Treasury Inspector General for Tax Administration (TIGTA) at www.treasury.gov/tigta and to the FTC.

5. **Block the Number:**

- She blocks the caller's number on her phone to prevent further calls.

***

Scenario 3: Identifying a Fake Charity

Situation:

Tom receives a phone call from a charity claiming to help disaster victims. The caller pressures him to donate immediately using his credit card.

Steps to Take:

1. **Research the Charity:**

   - Tom asks for the charity's website and registration number, then tells the caller he will donate online if interested.

2. **Verify the Charity's Legitimacy:**

   - He researches the charity on websites like Charity Navigator and the BBB Wise Giving Alliance to verify its legitimacy.

3. **Look for Red Flags:**

- Tom finds that the charity does not exist on these reputable sites and the caller's urgency is a red flag.

4. **Report the Call:**

- He reports the suspicious charity call to the FTC and his state's charity regulator.

5. **Consider Legitimate Donations:**

- If Tom still wishes to donate, he chooses a well-known and verified charity to support disaster victims.

Scenario 4: Dealing with a Tech Support Scam

Situation:
Susan's computer suddenly shows a pop-up message claiming that her system is infected with malware. The message urges her to call a tech support number immediately.

Steps to Take:

1. **Do Not Call the Number:**

   ○ Susan avoids calling the number provided in the pop-up message.

2. **Close the Pop-Up Safely:**

   ○ She tries to close the pop-up window. If it doesn't close, she uses Task Manager (Ctrl+Shift+Esc) to end the browser process.

3. **Run a Security Scan:**

   ○ Susan runs a full scan using her antivirus software to check for actual infections.

4. **Update Security Software:**

   ○ She ensures her antivirus and antimalware software are up to date.

5. **Report the Scam:**

   ○ Susan reports the tech support scam to the FTC and the software company mentioned in the pop-up.

6. **Educate Herself on Tech Support Scams:**

- ○ She reads more about tech support scams on the FTC's website to avoid falling for similar tactics in the future.

Scenario 5: Recognizing and Avoiding Investment Scams

Situation:
David receives an unsolicited email offering a "once-in-a-lifetime" investment opportunity with guaranteed high returns. The sender claims to have inside information and pressures David to invest quickly.

Steps to Take:

1. **Be Skeptical of Unsolicited Offers:**

- ○ David is wary of unsolicited investment offers, especially those promising guaranteed returns.

2. Research the Investment:

- He searches online for information about the investment and the company offering it. He finds multiple warnings about similar scams.

3. Consult with a Financial Advisor:

- David discusses the offer with his financial advisor, who advises him against investing in unsolicited opportunities.

4. Report the Email:

- David forwards the email to the FTC and reports it to the Securities and Exchange Commission (SEC) at www.sec.gov.

5. Avoid Further Communication:

- He deletes the email and blocks the sender to avoid any further contact.

***

Scenario 6: Responding to a Romance Scam

Situation:

Linda meets someone on a dating site who quickly expresses strong feelings for her and starts asking for money, claiming to need it for an emergency.

Steps to Take:

1. **Be Cautious of Fast-Moving Relationships:**

   - Linda is cautious about someone who expresses strong emotions quickly and asks for money.

2. **Research the Person:**

   - She searches online for information about the person and finds reports of similar scams.

3. **Stop Communication:**

   - Linda stops communicating with the person and blocks them on the dating site.

4. **Report the Scam:**

- She reports the scam to the dating site and the FTC.

5. **Educate Herself on Romance Scams:**

   - Linda reads more about romance scams on the FTC's website to recognize and avoid them in the future.

***

Scenario 7: Avoiding Lottery and Sweepstakes Scams

Situation:
Brian receives a letter claiming he has won a large sum of money in a foreign lottery. To claim his prize, he must pay a processing fee upfront.

Steps to Take:

1. **Recognize Red Flags:**

   - Brian knows he didn't enter any foreign lottery and is skeptical of the unsolicited letter.

2. **Research the Lottery:**

   ○ He searches for information about the lottery and finds it listed as a common scam.

3. **Avoid Sending Money:**

   ○ Brian does not send any money or provide personal information.

4. **Report the Letter:**

   ○ He reports the scam to the FTC and the U.S. Postal Inspection Service.

5. **Warn Others:**

   ○ Brian shares his experience with friends and family to warn them about similar scams.

Scenario 8: Handling a Fake Job Offer

Situation:

Sarah receives an email offering her a high-paying job with minimal requirements. The employer asks for her personal information and a fee for processing her application.

Steps to Take:

1. **Be Skeptical of Unsolicited Offers:**

   - Sarah is cautious about unsolicited job offers, especially those that seem too good to be true.

2. **Research the Company:**

   - She searches online for information about the company and finds numerous complaints and warnings about job scams.

3. **Avoid Providing Personal Information:**

   - Sarah does not provide any personal information or send money.

4. **Report the Offer:**

   - She reports the fake job offer to the FTC

and the job board where the offer was posted.

5. **Look for Legitimate Opportunities:**

   - Sarah uses reputable job boards and verifies companies through their official websites before applying.

Scenario 9: Identifying a Utility Scam

Situation:
Mark receives a call from someone claiming to be from his utility company, stating that his account is past due and he must pay immediately to avoid service disconnection.

Steps to Take:

1. **Do Not Provide Payment Information:**

   - Mark does not provide any payment information over the phone.

2. **Verify the Caller:**

- He tells the caller he will call back and hangs up. Mark then looks up his utility company's official phone number.

3. **Contact the Utility Company Directly:**

- Mark calls the utility company using the number on his bill to verify his account status. The company confirms that his account is in good standing and the call was a scam.

4. **Report the Call:**

- He reports the scam call to his utility company and the FTC.

5. **Educate Himself on Utility Scams:**

- Mark reads more about utility scams on his utility company's website to recognize and avoid them in the future.

Scenario 10: Dealing with a Social Media Scam

Situation:

Emma receives a message on social media from a friend, claiming they are in trouble and need money urgently. The message includes a link to send money through a wire transfer service.

Steps to Take:

1. **Verify the Friend's Situation:**

   - Emma contacts her friend directly through a phone call or another trusted method to verify if they are really in trouble.

2. **Do Not Click on Links:**

   - She avoids clicking on any links in the message.

3. **Report the Message:**

   - Emma reports the suspicious message to the social media platform and warns her friend that their account may have been hacked.

4. **Educate Herself on Social Media Scams:**

- She reads more about social media scams on the FTC's website to recognize and avoid them in the future.

5. **Strengthen Security:**

- Emma advises her friend to change their social media passwords and enable two-factor authentication to secure their account.

Scenario 11: Responding to a Grandparent Scam

Situation:
Paul receives a frantic phone call from someone claiming to be his grandson, stating that they are in trouble and need money urgently for bail. The caller asks Paul not to tell anyone and to send money via wire transfer.

Steps to Take:

1. **Stay Calm and Do Not Send Money:**

   - Paul remains calm and does not send any money.

2. **Verify the Caller's Identity:**

   - He asks the caller questions that only his real grandson would know. Paul then contacts his grandson or another family member directly to verify the situation.

3. **Report the Call:**

   - After confirming that his grandson is safe, Paul reports the scam call to the FTC and his local law enforcement.

4. **Warn Other Family Members:**

   - Paul informs his family about the scam to prevent them from falling victim to similar calls.

5. **Educate Himself on Grandparent Scams:**

   - He reads more about grandparent scams on the FTC's website to recognize and avoid them in the future.

Scenario 12: Dealing with a Health Insurance Scam

Situation:

Laura receives a call from someone claiming to be from her health insurance company, stating that her policy is being canceled unless she provides her personal information immediately.

Steps to Take:

1. **Do Not Provide Personal Information:**

   ◦ Laura does not provide any personal information over the phone.

2. **Verify the Caller:**

   ◦ She tells the caller she will call back and hangs up. Laura then looks up her health insurance company's official phone number.

3. **Contact the Insurance Company Directly:**

   ◦ Laura calls the insurance company using
   the number on her insurance card to verify
   her policy status. The company confirms
   that her policy is active and the call was a
   scam.

4. **Report the Call:**

   ◦ She reports the scam call to her insurance
   company and the FTC.

5. **Educate Herself on Health Insurance
   Scams:**

   ◦ Laura reads more about health insurance
   scams on the FTC's website to recognize
   and avoid them in the future.

***

Scenario 13: Avoiding Home Repair Scams

Situation:

Mike is approached by a contractor offering a great deal on home repairs, claiming they have extra materials from a nearby job and can start immediately. The contractor requests a large upfront payment.

Steps to Take:

1. **Research the Contractor:**

   ○ Mike asks for the contractor's license number, business card, and references.

2. **Check Reviews and References:**

   ○ He searches online for reviews and checks the contractor's references. Mike finds negative reviews and complaints about the contractor.

3. **Verify Credentials:**

   ○ Mike checks the contractor's license status with his state's licensing board and finds it is not valid.

4. **Avoid Upfront Payments:**

◦ He decides not to provide any upfront payment or sign any contracts.

5. **Report the Contractor:**

◦ Mike reports the suspicious contractor to the BBB and his state's consumer protection agency.

6. **Hire a Reputable Contractor:**

◦ Mike hires a contractor with verified credentials, positive reviews, and a valid license.

Scenario 14: Spotting an Investment Seminar Scam

Situation:
Karen receives an invitation to a free investment seminar promising high returns with little risk. The seminar requires her to sign up with her personal information and make an initial investment to secure her spot.

Steps to Take:

1. **Research the Seminar:**

   - Karen searches for information about the seminar and the speakers online. She finds mixed reviews and some warnings about the legitimacy of the event.

2. **Consult with a Financial Advisor:**

   - She discusses the seminar with her financial advisor, who advises caution and suggests verifying the credentials of the speakers and the company hosting the seminar.

3. **Avoid Sharing Personal Information:**

   - Karen does not provide any personal or financial information when signing up.

4. **Attend with Caution:**

   - If Karen decides to attend, she does so without committing any money or sharing sensitive information.

5. **Report Suspicious Activity:**

   - If the seminar turns out to be a high-pressure sales event or a scam, Karen reports it to the FTC and the SEC.

6. **Continue Education:**

   - Karen reads more about investment scams on the SEC's website to recognize and avoid similar situations in the future.

Seven

Frequently Asked Questions

♥

In the realm of cybersecurity and fraud prevention, there are many common questions and concerns that people often have. This Frequently Asked Questions (FAQs) section aims to address these concerns by providing clear, concise answers and practical advice. This chapter is designed to help you deepen your understanding, clarify any uncertainties, and equip you with the knowledge needed to stay safe in an increasingly digital world.

These FAQs serve as a quick reference guide for common concerns and questions about scams, identity theft, and cybersecurity. They offer practical tips, clarify misunderstandings, and provide straightforward answers to help you navigate complex topics. By addressing these frequently asked questions, you gain a deeper understanding of how to protect yourself and what steps to take if you encounter a threat.

Scope of This Chapter

This chapter covers a wide range of frequently asked questions related to scams, identity theft, and cybersecurity. Topics include:

- **Recognizing Phishing Attempts**

- **Responding to Suspicious Phone Calls**

- **Protecting Yourself from Identity Theft**

- **Steps to Take if You Are a Victim of Identity Theft**

- **Verifying the Legitimacy of Charities**

- **Identifying Common Scam Red Flags**

- **Protecting Your Online Accounts**

- **Actions to Take if You Fall for a Scam**

How to Use This Chapter

Use the FAQs section as a quick reference guide whenever you have a question or concern about cybersecurity and fraud prevention. Whether you are unsure about the legitimacy of an email, need advice on securing your online accounts, or want to know what steps to take if you suspect identity theft, this chapter provides the answers you need.

Empowering Yourself Through Knowledge

By familiarizing yourself with these FAQs, you em-power yourself to take proactive measures to pro-tect your personal information and stay safe from scams and fraud. Knowledge is a powerful tool in the fight against cyber threats, and this chapter aims to equip you with the information you need to stay vigilant and secure.

FAQ 1: How can I tell if an email is a phishing attempt?

Phishing emails often look legitimate but contain subtle signs that indicate they are fraudulent. Here are some tips to help you identify phishing emails:

1. **Check the Sender's Email Address:**

   - Phishing emails often come from addresses that look similar to legitimate ones but may contain extra characters or misspellings.

   - **Example:** An email from "customersupport@bankxyzz.com" instead of "support@bankxyz.com".

2. **Look for Generic Greetings:**

   ○ Phishing emails often use generic greetings like "Dear Customer" instead of your name.

   ○ **Example:** "Dear Valued Customer" instead of "Dear John Smith".

3. **Examine the Content for Urgency and Threats:**

   ○ Phishing emails often create a sense of urgency or threaten consequences to prompt immediate action.

   ○ **Example:** "Your account will be suspended if you do not verify your information within 24 hours."

4. **Check for Spelling and Grammar Errors:**

   ○ Many phishing emails contain spelling and grammar mistakes.

   ○ **Example:** "We need to verify your account informations."

5. **Hover Over Links:**

- Hover your mouse over links to see the actual URL. Phishing emails often use links that look legitimate but lead to fraudulent websites.

- **Example:** A link that says "www.bankxyz.com" but actually leads to "www.my-site.com".

FAQ 2: What should I do if I receive a suspicious phone call?

If you receive a suspicious phone call, follow these steps:

1. **Do Not Provide Personal Information:**

   - Avoid giving out any personal or financial information over the phone.

2. **Verify the Caller's Identity:**

   - Ask for the caller's name, department, and

a callback number. Verify the information by contacting the organization directly using a known phone number.

3. **Hang Up If Unsure:**

   ◦ If you are unsure about the legitimacy of the call, hang up and verify the information independently.

4. **Report the Call:**

   ◦ Report the suspicious call to the FTC and, if applicable, to the organization the caller claimed to represent.

5. **Block the Number:**

   ◦ Use your phone's call-blocking feature to block the number and prevent further calls.

***

FAQ 3: How can I protect myself from identity theft?

Here are some steps you can take to protect yourself from identity theft:

1. **Use Strong, Unique Passwords:**

   - Create strong passwords for your online accounts and avoid using the same password for multiple accounts. Consider using a password manager to keep track of your passwords.

2. **Enable Two-Factor Authentication (2FA):**

   - Enable 2FA on your accounts to add an extra layer of security.

3. **Monitor Your Accounts Regularly:**

   - Check your bank and credit card statements regularly for unauthorized transactions.

4. **Shred Sensitive Documents:**

   - Shred documents containing personal information before disposing of them.

5. **Secure Your Devices:**

- Use antivirus software and keep your devices updated with the latest security patches.

6. **Be Cautious with Personal Information:**

- Avoid sharing personal information over the phone, through email, or on social media.

***

FAQ 4: What should I do if I suspect I'm a victim of identity theft?

If you suspect you are a victim of identity theft, take these steps immediately:

1. **Contact Financial Institutions:**

- Notify your bank, credit card companies, and other financial institutions. Request that they close or freeze affected accounts.

2. **Place a Fraud Alert:**

- Contact one of the three major credit bureaus (Equifax, Experian, TransUnion) to place a fraud alert on your credit report.

3. **File a Report with the FTC:**

- Use the FTC's IdentityTheft.gov website to report the identity theft and create a recovery plan.

4. **File a Police Report:**

- Report the identity theft to your local police department and provide them with a copy of your FTC report.

5. **Monitor Your Credit Reports:**

- Regularly check your credit reports for any unauthorized activity or new accounts you did not open.

FAQ 5: How can I verify if a charity is legitimate?

To verify if a charity is legitimate, follow these steps:

1. **Research the Charity:**

   - Look up the charity on websites like Charity Navigator, GuideStar, and the BBB Wise Giving Alliance.

2. **Check for Registration:**

   - Verify that the charity is registered with the appropriate state charity regulator.

3. **Ask for Information:**

   - Contact the charity directly and ask for detailed information about their mission, programs, and finances.

4. **Look for Red Flags:**

   - Be cautious of charities that pressure you to donate immediately or are vague about how donations are used.

5. **Verify Contact Information:**

   - Ensure the charity's contact information

matches what is listed on their official website.

FAQ 6: What are common red flags of a scam?

Common red flags of a scam include:

1. **Urgency and Pressure:**

    ◦ Scammers create a sense of urgency to prompt immediate action without thinking.

2. **Requests for Personal Information:**

    ◦ Legitimate organizations typically do not ask for sensitive information through unsolicited calls or emails.

3. **Unsolicited Offers or Prizes:**

    ◦ Be cautious of unsolicited messages or calls claiming you have won a prize or offer you did not apply for.

4. **Too Good to Be True:**

   ◦ Offers that seem too good to be true often
     are.

5. **Unusual Payment Methods:**

   ◦ Scammers often request payments via un-
     conventional methods, such as gift cards
     or wire transfers.

6. **Emotional Manipulation:**

   ◦ Scammers use emotional appeals to ma-
     nipulate you into making decisions based
     on feelings rather than logic.

FAQ 7: How can I protect my online ac-
counts?

Here are some tips to protect your online accounts:

1. **Use Strong Passwords:**

   - Create complex passwords using a mix of letters, numbers, and special characters. Avoid using easily guessable information like birthdays.

2. **Enable Two-Factor Authentication (2FA):**

   - Add an extra layer of security by enabling 2FA on your accounts.

3. **Monitor Account Activity:**

   - Regularly check your account activity for any unauthorized transactions or changes.

4. **Be Cautious with Emails and Links:**

   - Avoid clicking on links or downloading attachments from unknown or suspicious emails.

5. **Update Security Settings:**

   - Adjust your account settings to maximize privacy and security, such as enabling login alerts and restricting third-party app access.

6. **Use Antivirus Software:**

   ○ Install and update antivirus software to protect against malware and other online threats.

***

FAQ 8: What should I do if I fall for a scam?

If you fall for a scam, take these steps immediately:

1. **Stop Communication:**

   ○ Cease all communication with the scammer.

2. **Report the Scam:**

   ○ Report the scam to the FTC, your financial institutions, and any other relevant authorities.

3. **Monitor Accounts:**

   ○ Check your bank and credit card statements for unauthorized transactions.

4. **Change Passwords:**

- ○ Change the passwords for any accounts that may have been compromised.

5. **Seek Support:**

- ○ Reach out to friends, family, or support groups for emotional and practical support.

6. **Educate Yourself:**

- ○ Learn about common scams to avoid falling for similar schemes in the future.

Eight

Conclusion

♥

Congratulations on reaching the end of this comprehensive guide on how to protect yourself from scams and fraud. By now, you have gained valuable knowledge on various types of scams, learned practical steps to enhance your security, and explored real-life scenarios that illustrate how to apply what you've learned. This chapter will summarize key points, reinforce important takeaways, and provide final tips to keep you safe in the digital world.

Key Takeaways

- **Awareness is Your First Line of Defense:**

  - Staying informed about common scams and fraud tactics is crucial. Regularly update your knowledge to recognize new threats as they emerge. Awareness helps you recognize red flags and avoid potential pitfalls.

- **Be Skeptical and Verify Information:**

  - Always verify the legitimacy of unsolicited requests for personal information, whether they come via email, phone, or mail. Trust but verify. Being skeptical and cautious can prevent you from falling victim to scams.

- **Protect Personal Information:**

  - Be cautious about sharing personal and financial information. Use strong, unique passwords and enable two-factor authentication on your accounts. Protecting your personal information is essential for maintaining your privacy and security.

- **Report Suspicious Activity:**

  - Reporting scams and fraudulent activity to the appropriate authorities helps track and combat these threats, protecting others in the process. Your actions can contribute to broader efforts to prevent and address scams.

- **Utilize Available Resources:**

  - Take advantage of the numerous resources and tools available, such as identity theft protection services, secure browsing tools, and educational websites. Utilizing these resources enhances your ability to stay safe and informed.

Final Tips for Staying Safe

- **Regularly Monitor Accounts:**

  - Check your bank and credit card statements regularly for any unauthorized transactions. Early detection is key to minimizing damage. Consistently monitoring your accounts helps you catch and address issues promptly.

- **Update Security Measures:**

  ○ Ensure your antivirus software, operating system, and applications are always up to date to protect against the latest threats. Regular updates enhance your devices' security and protect you from emerging threats.

- **Educate and Share:**

  ○ Share what you've learned with friends and family to help them stay safe as well. Education is a powerful tool in the fight against fraud. By spreading knowledge, you contribute to a more informed and secure community.

- **Stay Calm and Act Quickly:**

  ○ If you suspect you have been targeted by a scam, stay calm and take immediate action. Follow the steps outlined in this guide to respond effectively. Prompt action can mitigate the impact of scams and protect your assets.

- **Seek Support When Needed:**

  - Dealing with scams and identity theft can be stressful. Don't hesitate to seek support from trusted individuals or professional counselors if needed. Emotional support is important in navigating the challenges posed by scams and fraud.

Looking Ahead

The digital landscape is continually evolving, and so are the tactics used by scammers. Staying vigilant and proactive in your approach to security will help you navigate this ever-changing environment safely. Remember, the knowledge and tools you've gained from this guide are your best defense against fraud and scams.

Building a Stronger Community

- **Community Awareness:**

  - Encourage community discussions about scams and fraud prevention. Sharing experiences and knowledge within your community can create a supportive network that helps everyone stay informed and protected.

- **Support Networks:**

  - Join or form support networks for individuals who have experienced scams or identity theft. These networks provide a platform for sharing advice, resources, and emotional support, helping victims recover and prevent future incidents.

- **Advocacy:**

  - Advocate for stronger regulations and policies to combat scams and fraud. Participate in initiatives that promote consumer protection and push for enhanced measures to safeguard personal information.

Empowering Yourself and Others

- **Continuous Learning:**

  - Stay updated on the latest scams and cybersecurity trends. Subscribe to newsletters, attend webinars, and read articles from reputable sources to ensure you are always informed about new threats and prevention strategies.

- **Proactive Measures:**

  - Implement proactive measures such as regular security audits, password management, and cautious online behavior. Being proactive minimizes your risk of falling victim to scams and enhances your overall security.

- **Sharing Knowledge:**

  - Share your knowledge with others, especially those who may be more vulnerable to scams, such as seniors and less tech-savvy individuals. Your guidance can make a significant difference in their ability to protect themselves.

- **Mentor and Educate:**

  - Use your knowledge to mentor others, particularly those who may be more vulnerable to scams. Host informational sessions or casual discussions to share what you've learned.

- **Create Awareness Campaigns:**

  - Partner with local organizations or community groups to create awareness campaigns about common scams and fraud prevention techniques. Distributing flyers, hosting seminars, or using social media can help spread the word.

- **Advocate for Stronger Protections:**

  - Support initiatives and policies that aim to strengthen consumer protections against scams and fraud. Your voice can contribute to broader efforts to create a safer environment for everyone.

Additional Resources

For ongoing education and support, consider the following resources:

- **Federal Trade Commission (FTC):** www.ftc.gov

- **IdentityTheft.gov:** www.identitytheft.gov

- **Better Business Bureau (BBB):** www.bbb.org

- **Consumer Financial Protection Bureau (CFPB):** www.consumerfinance.gov

- **AARP Fraud Watch Network:** www.aarp.org/money/scams-fraud/

Continuing Your Education

- **Stay Updated:**

  - Regularly check reputable sources for the latest information on scams and cybersecurity threats. Subscribing to newsletters from trusted organizations like the FTC or

AARP can provide you with timely updates and tips.

- **Engage in Ongoing Learning:**

  - Consider attending workshops, webinars, or community events focused on cybersecurity and fraud prevention. These events can offer deeper insights and practical advice.

- **Read Books and Articles:**

  - Explore additional literature on cybersecurity and fraud prevention. Many books and articles provide in-depth analysis and strategies to protect yourself in the digital age.

Maintaining Your Vigilance

- **Regular Security Audits:**

  - Periodically review your security practices and update them as needed. Ensure your devices, accounts, and personal information are adequately protected.

- **Stay Skeptical:**

  - Maintain a healthy level of skepticism, especially when dealing with unsolicited offers or requests for personal information. Trust your instincts and verify information before taking action.

- **Foster a Culture of Security:**

  - Encourage those around you to adopt good security habits. A collective effort can significantly enhance overall safety and reduce the likelihood of falling victim to scams.

Final Thoughts

The journey to protecting yourself from scams and fraud is ongoing. As you continue to apply the knowledge and strategies outlined in this guide, you will become more adept at recognizing and responding to threats. Your commitment to staying informed and vigilant is the best defense against the evolving landscape of scams and fraud.

Remember, you are not alone in this journey. Support networks, educational resources, and community initiatives are there to assist you. Together, we can create a safer and more secure environment for everyone.

Thank you once again for your dedication to learning and safeguarding your digital life. Stay safe, stay informed, and continue to empower yourself and others in the fight against scams and fraud. Next up are some quizzes!

Nine

Quizes

Quiz 1: Phishing Scams

Questions:

1. What is a common characteristic of a phishing email?

    ◦ a) Personalized greeting

    ◦ b) Generic greeting like "Dear Customer"

    ◦ c) No greeting at all

2. Which of the following is a red flag in a phishing email?

    ◦ a) Spelling and grammar errors

- b) High-quality graphics

- c) Properly spelled words and correct grammar

3. What should you do if you receive a suspicious email?

  - a) Click on the link to verify

  - b) Delete it without taking any action

  - c) Report it to your email provider and the FTC

4. Phishing emails often create a sense of:

  - a) Calm

  - b) Urgency

  - c) Relaxation

5. How can you verify the legitimacy of an email sender?

  - a) Click the link in the email

  - b) Reply to the email

- ○ c) Contact the company directly using information from their official website

Answers:

1. b) Generic greeting like "Dear Customer"

2. a) Spelling and grammar errors

3. c) Report it to your email provider and the FTC

4. b) Urgency

5. c) Contact the company directly using information from their official website

Quiz 2: Phone Scams

Questions:

1. If you receive a suspicious call demanding immediate payment, what should you do first?

    ◦ a) Provide your payment information

    ◦ b) Hang up and verify the call independently

    ◦ c) Stay on the line and ask for more details

2. What is a common tactic used by phone scammers?

    ◦ a) Asking for your full name

    ◦ b) Creating a sense of urgency or fear

    ◦ c) Offering free gifts

3. Which payment method is often requested by phone scammers?

    ◦ a) Credit card

- b) Wire transfer or gift cards

- c) Check

4. What should you do if a caller claims to be from the IRS and threatens you with arrest?

  - a) Provide your Social Security number

  - b) Hang up and contact the IRS directly

  - c) Ask for the caller's supervisor

5. How can you block further calls from a known scam number?

  - a) Answer the call and ask them to stop

  - b) Use your phone's call-blocking feature

  - c) Change your phone number

Answers:

1. b) Hang up and verify the call independently

2. b) Creating a sense of urgency or fear

3. b) Wire transfer or gift cards

4. b) Hang up and contact the IRS directly

5. b) Use your phone's call-blocking feature

Quiz 3: Fake Charities

Questions:

1. Before donating to a charity, you should:

   ○ a) Send money immediately if they claim it's urgent

   ○ b) Research the charity on sites like Charity Navigator

   ○ c) Trust their word without verification

2. What is a red flag when evaluating a charity?

   ○ a) Clear explanation of how donations are used

   ○ b) Pressure to donate immediately

   ○ c) Registered with the state charity regulator

3. How can you verify if a charity is legitimate?

   ○ a) Ask the caller for their personal information

- b) Research the charity on reputable sites

- c) Donate small amounts first to test them

4. A legitimate charity will:

- a) Pressure you for immediate donations

- b) Provide clear and transparent information about their work

- c) Only accept cash donations

5. If you suspect a charity scam, you should:

- a) Ignore it and move on

- b) Report it to the FTC and your state charity regulator

- c) Donate to avoid trouble

Answers:

1. b) Research the charity on sites like Charity Navigator

2. b) Pressure to donate immediately

3. b) Research the charity on reputable sites

4. b) Provide clear and transparent information about their work

5. b) Report it to the FTC and your state charity regulator

Quiz 4: Tech Support Scams

Questions:

1. What is a common sign of a tech support scam?

   ◦ a) Unsolicited pop-up messages claiming your computer is infected

   ◦ b) Receiving an email from your known tech support provider

   ◦ c) Getting a call from a friend about tech issues

2. What should you do if you receive a suspicious pop-up message on your computer?

   ◦ a) Call the provided tech support number

   ◦ b) Close the pop-up and run a security scan

   ◦ c) Follow the instructions in the pop-up

3. Tech support scammers often ask for:

   ◦ a) Remote access to your computer

- b) Your opinions on software

- c) Recommendations for antivirus software

4. To verify a legitimate tech support call, you should:

   - a) Provide your personal information

   - b) Contact the company directly using known contact details

   - c) Ask for a discount

5. If you fall for a tech support scam, you should:

   - a) Do nothing

   - b) Report it to the FTC and your antivirus provider

   - c) Pay them to avoid further issues

Answers:

1. a) Unsolicited pop-up messages claiming your computer is infected

2. b) Close the pop-up and run a security scan

3. a) Remote access to your computer

4. b) Contact the company directly using known contact details

5. b) Report it to the FTC and your antivirus provider

Quiz 5: Investment Scams

Questions:

1. An unsolicited email offering a high-return investment is likely:

   - a) A legitimate opportunity

   - b) An investment scam

   - c) A government bond

2. What is a common red flag in investment scams?

   - a) Guaranteed high returns with little or no risk

   - b) Detailed explanations of investment strategies

   - c) Requests for small, gradual investments

3. Before investing, you should:

   - a) Trust the email sender

- b) Research the investment and consult with a financial advisor

- c) Send money quickly to secure your spot

4. If an investment opportunity seems too good to be true, it:

- a) Is a rare chance

- b) Is probably a scam

- c) Should be grabbed immediately

5. After identifying an investment scam, you should:

- a) Report it to the SEC and the FTC

- b) Ignore it

- c) Invest a small amount to test

Answers:

1. b) An investment scam

2. a) Guaranteed high returns with little or no risk

3. b) Research the investment and consult with a financial advisor

4. b) Is probably a scam

5. a) Report it to the SEC and the FTC

Quiz 6: Romance Scams

Questions:

1. A common tactic used in romance scams is:

    ◦ a) Moving the relationship forward very quickly

    ◦ b) Asking about your favorite movies

    ◦ c) Sending you flowers

2. What should you do if someone you met online asks for money?

    ◦ a) Send it immediately if you care about them

    ◦ b) Stop communication and verify their story independently

    ◦ c) Trust them without question

3. How can you protect yourself from romance scams?

    ◦ a) Share your financial information early

- b) Keep personal details private and take things slowly

- c) Move the relationship offline quickly

4. If you suspect a romance scam, you should:

- a) Continue to communicate but be cautious

- b) Stop all communication and report the profile

- c) Send a small amount of money to test them

5. Scammers in romance scams often claim to be:

- a) Working abroad or in the military

- b) Living next door

- c) In financial trouble locally

Answers:

1. a) Moving the relationship forward very quickly

2. b) Stop communication and verify their story independently

3. b) Keep personal details private and take things slowly

4. b) Stop all communication and report the profile

5. a) Working abroad or in the military

Ten

Appendices

♥

Appendix A: Glossary of Terms

Understanding the terminology used in cybersecurity and fraud prevention is essential for staying informed and protected. This glossary provides definitions for common terms and concepts you may encounter.

- **Antivirus Software:** Programs designed to detect and remove malware from your computer.

- **Botnet:** A network of compromised computers controlled by a hacker.

- **Data Breach:** An incident where sensitive, protected, or confidential data is accessed or disclosed without authorization.

- **Encryption:** The process of converting information or data into a code to prevent unauthorized access.

- **Firewall:** A security system that monitors and controls incoming and outgoing network traffic based on predetermined security rules.

- **Identity Theft:** The fraudulent acquisition and use of a person's private identifying information, usually for financial gain.

- **Malware:** Malicious software designed to harm, exploit, or otherwise compromise the functioning of a computer system.

- **Phishing:** A method of trying to gather personal information using deceptive emails and websites.

- **Ransomware:** A type of malware that locks or encrypts data on a victim's computer, demanding payment to unlock or decrypt the data.

- **Spam:** Unsolicited and often irrelevant or inappropriate messages sent over the internet, typically to a large number of users.

Appendix B: Checklist for Online Safety

Use this checklist to ensure you are taking the necessary steps to protect yourself online.

1. **Use Strong Passwords:**

   - Create unique passwords for each of your accounts.

   - Use a mix of letters, numbers, and special characters.

   - Consider using a password manager.

2. **Enable Two-Factor Authentication (2FA):**

- Add an extra layer of security to your accounts by enabling 2FA.

3. **Update Software Regularly:**

- Keep your operating system, browser, and other software up to date with the latest security patches.

4. **Install Antivirus Software:**

- Use reputable antivirus software and keep it updated.

5. **Be Cautious with Emails and Links:**

- Avoid clicking on links or downloading attachments from unknown or suspicious emails.

6. **Secure Your Home Network:**

- Use a strong password for your Wi-Fi network.

- Enable network encryption (WPA3 is the most secure).

7. **Monitor Your Accounts:**

- Regularly check your bank and credit card statements for unauthorized transactions.

8. **Shred Sensitive Documents:**

- Shred documents containing personal information before disposing of them.

9. **Be Aware of Scams:**

- Stay informed about common scams and how to avoid them.

Appendix C: Quick Tips for Staying Safe

Here are some quick tips to help you stay safe from scams and fraud.

1. **Think Before You Click:**

- Be cautious of links and attachments in emails, especially from unknown senders.

2. **Verify Requests for Personal Information:**

   ○ Always verify the legitimacy of requests for personal or financial information.

3. **Use Secure Websites:**

   ○ Ensure websites use HTTPS, indicating a secure connection, before entering personal information.

4. **Educate Yourself:**

   ○ Stay informed about the latest scams and cybersecurity threats.

5. **Trust Your Instincts:**

   ○ If something feels off, it probably is. Trust your instincts and verify information.

Appendix D: Additional Resources

Here are some additional resources to help you stay informed and protected.

1. **Federal Trade Commission (FTC):**

   ◦ **Website:** www.ftc.gov

   ◦ **Phone:** 1-877-FTC-HELP (1-877-382-4357)

2. **IdentityTheft.gov:**

   ◦ **Website:** www.identitytheft.gov

3. **Better Business Bureau (BBB):**

   ◦ **Website:** www.bbb.org

4. **Consumer Financial Protection Bureau (CFPB):**

   ◦ **Website:** www.consumerfinance.gov

   ◦ **Phone:** 1-855-411-CFPB (1-855-411-2372)

5. **AARP Fraud Watch Network:**

   ◦ **Website:** www.aarp.org/money/scams-fraud/

6. **StaySafeOnline:**

   ◦ **Website:** www.staysafeonline.org

7. **National Cyber Security Alliance (NCSA):**

   ◦ **Website:** www.staysafeonline.org/national-cyber-security-alliance/

8. **Internet Crime Complaint Center (IC3):**

   ◦ **Website:** www.ic3.gov

9. **United States Postal Inspection Service (USPIS):**

   ◦ **Website:** www.uspis.gov

   ◦ **Phone:** 1-877-876-2455

www.ingramcontent.com/pod-product-compliance
Lightning Source LLC
Chambersburg PA
CBHW060857120626
46553CB00001B/123